Susan Abel Lieberman

New Traditions

REDEFINING CELEBRATIONS
FOR TODAY'S FAMILY

The Noonday Press
Farrar, Straus and Giroux
New York

Library of Congress Cataloging in Publication Data
Lieberman, Susan Abel.
New traditions : redefining celebrations for today's family /
Susan A. Lieberman.
p.   cm.
Published in 1984 under title: Let's celebrate.
1. Family—United States—Folklore.   2. Family festivals—United
States.   3. Holidays—United States.   I. Lieberman, Susan Abel.
Let's celebrate.   II. Title.
GR105.L495   1990   398'.0973—dc20   90-42997

New Traditions

To my husband, Michael,
and our sons, Seth and Jonathan,
for unending encouragement, enthusiasm,
laughter, and love

Acknowledgments for the Revised Edition

IT IS the fortunate author who has two chances with one book. *New Traditions* first appeared in 1984 as *Let's Celebrate: Creating New Family Traditions*, under the Perigee imprint. My thanks to my editor, Elisabeth Dyssegaard, and Farrar, Straus and Giroux for flouting conventional wisdom and bringing out this revised and expanded new edition. Elisabeth's gentle advice and energetic leadership have been much appreciated.

Barrie Van Dyck and Blanche Schlessinger, my agents, deserve both praise and thanks. They are persevering, capable, and wise; they are good friends.

Especially important to me are the people I met all over the country while researching and promoting this book who shared my interest in new traditions, offered their best ideas, and convinced me this book had an eager audience. I have loved meeting the many men and women who so willingly talked about their family lives and their personal needs. Their ideas and wisdom have enriched my own family and led us to satisfying moments of warmth, reverence, and reflection.

When, in 1983, I first wrote about Second-Stage Traditions, it was, for me, theory. Seven years later, with our older son about to leave for college and the younger hot on his heels, it is uncomfortable reality. I feel the need for new traditions just as much now as I did when I began this book.

CONTENTS

1. *Why We Need New Traditions and How to Get Them*   5

2. *Celebrating the Family*   15
    17 The Ritual Family Dinner
    19 No-Reason Parties
    21 The Family Walk
    23 Kneading Time
    25 The Family Cup
    26 The "You Are Special" Plate
    27 Once-a-Week Days
    31 Sunday-Night Bible Reading
    32 The Morning Circle
    34 Elder Evenings
    35 Car-Pool Wishes
    37 Your Turn
    37 Wishes for the World
    38 The Best Thing in the Week

3. *Religious Holidays*   43
    44 CHRISTMAS
    46 No-Surprise Christmas
    48 No Shopping in December
    50 Operation Fruitcake
    52 A Personal Christmas Tree
    53 All-Day Christmas
    55 Savoring the Season
    56 Happy Birthday, Jesus

Contents

57 The Family Service
58 HANUKKAH
58 The Hanukkah Plan
60 Light a New Menorah
61 EASTER
61 The Easter Nickel Hunt
62 Egg Ornaments
64 PASSOVER
64 The Passover Play

4. *Birthdays, Anniversaries, and Other Rites of Passage*   69
72 BIRTHDAYS
73 Coupon Birthdays
75 Summer-Winter Birthdays
76 Only-Me Birthday Dinners
77 Birthday Fairy
78 Clue Birthdays
79 Birthday Squares
82 Family Portraits
84 The Birthday Letter
85 ANNIVERSARIES
86 The Anniversary Fund
88 Plan a Fantasy
89 Every-Month Anniversaries
91 Come-Away-with-Me Anniversary
92 A Dating Game
93 BAR MITZVAH AND CONFIRMATION
93 Self-styled Bar Mitzvah
95 Tangible Affirmation
96 GRADUATION
96 Personal Diploma

5. *National Holidays*   101
102 The New Year's Annual Review Resolution
103 Mother as Guest
105 SOS Homemade Cards
107 Flowers, Candy, and Valentine's Escape
108 Stuffing the Photo Album

Contents

109 The Neighborhood Football Game
110 Thanksgiving Reading
112 A Family of Friends

6. *Single-Parent Traditions*   119

120 Guess Who's Coming to Dinner
121 Good-Morning Stories
122 Sin Night
123 Mother's Day / Father's Day Picnic
124 Reading Aloud
125 Do-It-Yourself Brunch
126 Birthday Potluck
127 The At-Home Vacation
128 Wednesday-Morning Pancakes

7. *Daddy Traditions*   133

134 Breakfast with Father
135 The Daddy Book
137 Dad's Trip
137 First Day / Last Day

8. *Second-Stage Traditions*   143

144 Reentry
144 Goodbye Blessings
145 The Christmas Fund
147 A Chair for the Missing
148 St. Nicholas Lives
149 The Family Letters
149 The Postcard Connection

9. *When There Is Just You*   157

158 Turf Time
158 Singles Hour
159 Gift of Self
160 Adopt-a-Family
161 Brunch Bunch
162 Always at My House
164 Matchmaking
164 The Travel Habit

Contents

166 Family Vacation
167 My Eyes Only
168 Kids Only
169 Compensations
170 Breakfast Club
170 Letter Writing
171 The X and Y Problem
172 Nuclear Family Weekend
172 Birthday Reflection

10. *Giving Traditions*   177
178 Lenten Giving
179 Fast Dinner
181 Tiny Volunteers

11. *How to Get Started*   187

Sharing: A Space for Your Best Ideas   195

New Traditions

1

Why We Need New Traditions and How to Get Them

OUR PACKED sixteen-wheel moving van arrived in St. Louis as America readied to celebrate her two hundredth birthday. The truck stopped in front of an imperturbable square of two-story brick which was not two hundred years old, but old enough to suggest permanence. This was a solid, secure, and inviting house. If it stretched us financially, it was a perfect fit emotionally.

Michael and I had been married eight years. We had, almost magically, acquired two children, five address changes, and 15,000 pounds of paraphernalia, all of which was in the van because we had grown comfortably attached to the stuff. It signified our growing commitment to family. We had everything we needed, it seemed, but roots; and with this house we would remedy that.

In pursuit of stability, we bought a rocking chair for the porch, a power mower for the grass, and a big table for the real dining room. Broke but delighted, we settled in to watch the children grow big enough to climb the back-yard apple tree, rake sweet gums off the lawn, and maneuver the heavy oak front door.

Domestic tranquillity was wrinkled by the realization that, amid all our possessions, something was missing. In the recesses of my mind lived a fiction-fed view of a bustling grandma baking cookies and a genial grandpa taking the boys fishing, of chestnuts by the roaring fire and picnics on the Fourth of July. Never mind that the kids don't like chestnuts, nobody likes picnics in July when it is 95 degrees with mosquitoes, and Grandma, now a thousand miles removed, never baked cookies.

Our extended family, so typical of mobile America, is scattered from Los Angeles to Miami. If the kids don't move, the parents do. It would, I calculated, cost $2,600 to have us all fly in to gather around the dining-room table—before the food.

Mobility pulls at family ties. I felt the stress keenly with each approaching holiday. Holidays are supposed to help us develop a clear sense of family identity. I wanted our children to grow up with Technicolor memories, with warm and cherished feelings. If holidays were special family times, I wanted them to be just that: special.

Instead, my holidays were heralded by a quiet sense of panic. My response was to take on holidays as my responsibility and to head for the kitchen. I equated making a holiday with cooking a holiday. And what I got, mostly, was dirty dishes.

The problem was further complicated by not wanting to stress an already fragile balance between competing forces in our lives. We were struggling to juggle Michael's career needs, my career needs, our personal aspirations, and the unceasing concerns for two small children. If life was rich with challenge and experience, it was short on psychic energy and sleep. We lived a fine line between sanity and hysteria. We very much needed the stability of family traditions.

How much I would have welcomed proscribed, comfortable patterns for celebrating important events. Traditions tell you how to make family times special. You don't have to worry about what to do or when to do it; you just do it. If only we had been better programmed, I thought, I could orchestrate these celebrations effortlessly. I could handle the work; it was the ambiguity that was unnerving.

Unfortunately, our own families were not tradition-rich. They relied on the talk-eat-and-unwrap method of celebration. This did not work so well with just four of us. But even our friends who had been more richly programmed seemed to be having trouble. Old traditions were not always congruent with their changing life-styles. There was pain in trying to force a fit. We all wanted family, warmth, and celebration. With mobility and careers and social pressures, we needed it more than ever.

Slowly came the notion of new tradition, of consciously and creatively establishing new family traditions designed to fit us.

How can traditions be *new*? Why not? If traditions help strengthen our sense of family but if the old traditions won't fit, adaptation is the logical response. Usually, it is an unconscious response. I believe modern life can be easier for us if we make the response conscious. When old traditions lose their vitality or cease to serve, we should unravel them and mix old threads with new to weave new family traditions that give us shared experiences and togetherness.

Sally Sabbatini Rosenfeld illustrates the point. Sally grew up in a house where her mother prepared homemade ravioli every Friday night. Papa Sabbatini played pinochle with neighborhood friends, who cheerfully swore at each other in Italian. Those Friday nights helped to define the Sabbatinis as family members, as Italian-Americans, and as members of the neighborhood. It was the way every week ended; and for Sally Sabbatini, it smelled good, tasted good, and felt good. But Sally Sabbatini Rosenfeld takes no pleasure in preparing homemade ravioli. Her husband, Roger, neither swears in Italian nor plays pinochle. It makes little sense for her children to define themselves as Italian. Neither does the very traditional Friday-evening Jewish Sabbath ritual of her husband's family fit comfortably. For the Rosenfelds, the traditional customs of their childhood ceased to work. It is questionable whether they would have continued even if Sally and Roger had had more similar backgrounds.

In the Rosenfelds' case there is a special need to integrate diverse backgrounds into a family life far more complex than that of the previous generation. But the Rosenfelds are not an isolated example. There are fewer clear external criteria of who we are. Church, neighborhood, ethnic group, or profession are less defining. Even men and women who marry from the same religious, economic, or social background find differences in how their families define themselves.

For many years Sally and Roger treated Friday no differently from any other night. But as the children grew, they began to discuss the need for more quiet, family-centered time in their lives, and those Friday evenings of childhood kept signaling just the sort of feelings they were looking for in the present.

Why does it have to be ravioli? thought Sally. She and Roger used a shared interest in wine and politics as their starting point in carving a special family time. Together, they made a commitment to reserve Friday evenings for themselves and their children. Roger brings home a new wine or an old favorite, which helps to make the evening special for him and Sally. For the children, it is the only night there are soft drinks with dinner. There is always a family discussion about a moral issue taken from the news.

At first, it was an effort to resist other temptations. The children were angry when they, too, had to turn down invitations. But, slowly, the pleasure of the evening took hold. Mark Rosenfeld, age nine, learned a little about grape growing, the geography of France, the history of Iran, and the structure of the Pentagon. More important, he came to look forward to the sense of specialness and togetherness that Sally and Roger created by establishing a pattern, a ritual in their weekly lives.

"Every Friday is not magic," says Roger. "Sometimes I am tired and cranky and impatient to stretch out alone. Sometimes Sally and I have obligations on Friday that we decide are important. But more often than not, it is a good time, a peaceful spot in the week. I look forward to it."

For the Rosenfelds, theirs is a new tradition born of old patterns that filled a vacuum in their lives. Warmth and togetherness grew slowly as habit took hold and tradition emerged.

Just what is tradition? Most of us know it as behavior handed down from one generation to the next, usually by word of mouth or by example. It is so accepted by us as almost to have the force of law, yet it need not be widely shared by others. Tradition often has religious implications, but many traditions are not religious. Frequently, there are accompanying rituals.

Ritual is more religious in nature than tradition and almost always solemn. Ritual dictates a prescribed order of performance. It codifies behavior and sanctifies it, thus helping us to know how to act in difficult times. Traditions allow more room for adaptation and experimentation. Tradition may have associated ritual, but traditions can be repetitive without being ritualistic.

It is easy to confuse tradition and custom. Custom is what is habitual, regular. Things we usually do that lots of other people usually do are likely to be customs. Customs are transmitted culturally. Traditions remain more personal and peculiar. I see traditions as weightier, more significant, more special for the users.

In a chaotic world in which change is the order of the day, tradition is a ballast, a comfortable and steady marker through the years. It punctuates time, like commas and periods, and makes us pause to order the contents of our lives. Tradition is family insurance against outside pressures that threaten to overwhelm our days and weaken our ties to one another. We do not have to invest energy and time in deciding what to do. We know what to do. With the weight of permanence and the force of habit, tradition demands our attention.

We Liebermans needed new traditions.

Later, in talking about this book, I found we were far from alone. Our feelings about tradition struck responsive chords in others who were also struggling with shaping family life. In hundreds of interviews, no one argued against the value of family traditions.

I began by talking with friends and then friends of friends and worked informally in widening circles, looking for families' best new traditions, for good ideas to help bond families together. Most of the people I interviewed are middle-class or upper-middle-class. Many are academics, professionals, or business people. In choosing traditions, however, I looked for those that did not depend on special affluence or position.

Names and personal details have been changed for privacy. Some traditions are composites; a few were reconstructed from second- or third-hand sources. But most are recounted just as they were told to me in living rooms or kitchens.

The result is a recipe book quite unlike anything I used for cooking for my earlier holidays. These are recipes for people's most creative, most effective, most valued new traditions. They are meant to help all kinds of families who share these needs: conventional families, single parents, dual-career couples, blended families, single people, and chaotic households everywhere struggling to maintain some very old-fashioned values in the context of newfangled life-styles.

For those who do not have satisfying traditions to pass on from generation to generation, why not pass them from one family to another? Some may fit your family exactly. You need not be Jewish to adopt the Gift-of-Self Night Hanukkah tradition, or a working mother to institute Sin Night. But most will work better with your own adaptation.

We light candles in our house on Friday night and say, "May peace and joy come to this home and to the homes of those we love, all week long." May traditions, new and old, bring peace and joy to your home, too.

2

Celebrating the Family

I ALWAYS FEEL that I am switching mental hats in the car on the way to being late or guilty. Between running meetings, taking classes, and driving car pools, the modern woman is supposed to communicate openly with her spouse, affirm her kids' dignity, unleash her full sexual potential, and jog. Modern man has all the usual pressures to succeed at work, regardless of an inflationary and tumultuous economy, and much more than his father, he is expected to share in family maintenance and nurturing. He is having to learn new rules in the middle of the game, and change can be difficult. Life gets very hectic.

Coping comes by ordering priorities. We do the essentials and let go of ironed undershorts, homemade pie crusts, or whatever Mother did that no longer feels important. Men discard chauvinistic stereotypes about what they should or should not do. Still, family traditions can be a problem. We do not want to give them up, like ironing undershorts; we cannot buy them ready-made, like pie crusts. Sometimes we hang on, halfheartedly, to unsatisfying behavior because we have nothing to substitute but a guilty feeling.

It helps to understand that there are some very practical reasons why traditions create problems. Many traditions presume a mother who does not work outside the home or a nuclear family in close proximity to the extended family. A good portion of American family tradition presumes an active involvement with church or ethnic community. Even more fundamental, many family traditions presume a shared commitment to a set of beliefs that is no longer common to all members of the extended family.

Finally, traditions, by definition, carry our past into our present. If we are fearful of or angry at our past, these traditions call up pain and hurt.

Changing life-styles frequently carry us physically or emotionally far from our families. While we value our changes and our gains, we can be left with emotional holes.

The busier our lives, the harder to figure out how to fill those holes. But the busier we are, the more important it is that we make sure there is special family time. It is not enough to think family is important; it must *be* important. What we do is the visible expression of our real values.

What we do, however, does not have to be done to someone else's time clock. Christmas, I realized, was not our best holiday to be nuclear, and the Fourth of July was not the best time to picnic in St. Louis. One family has its Fourth of July picnic on Christmas Eve, in front of the fire, with fried chicken on a red-and-white tablecloth. Another has its annual gathering of the clan, gifts and all, every Fourth of July.

Some of the most special new traditions that families share are not cued by the calendar. Unrelated to religious or national holidays, they are personal ways of saying "We are important," personal responses for their particular lives. The twelve new traditions in this chapter are examples of ways to celebrate the importance of family.

The Ritual Family Dinner

One of my favorite traditions took shape on an airplane over the Atlantic. It is important because it shows how simple words and simple gestures create powerful feelings. Here is a ritual any family can create for itself.

Gordon and Susan Toum were flying home from their first trip to Europe, a week in London. "We loved it," said Gordon. "It overwhelmed us with the presence of history and wealth of tradition. On the long flight back, we tried to encapsulate and assimilate what we had seen, what we felt. We had gone to the play *Fiddler on the Roof* one night while we were there and Tevye's cry 'Tradition, tradition . . .' kept echoing in our minds."

The Toums were coming home to St. Louis, but it was barely home then. They had only recently left Colorado, where they had grown up, gone to school, fallen in love, and married. Gordon had finished medical school; Susan had struggled to earn a master's degree in music; and each of their three children was born there. "When we lived in Colorado, the normal commotion of extended family kept us from thinking much about tradition, but after we moved, after we were separated from both the warmth and the rules of our own families, we began to question what we wanted. Religion was not an important part of our lives, and we did not have special family customs that we followed. We sort of floated along," said Gordon. "On the trip home, our senses heightened by excitement and fatigue, the idea of the family dinner took shape." By the time the plane touched ground, Gordon had written the words, the ritual reading, that the Toums have spoken at the Toum family dinners ever since.

"This is a very special dinner. We set the table as well as we can, the food is special, and we are dressed in our best clothes; it is a serious event. Special symbols are put on the table. There is the Toum family Bible, the oldest thing we own, a symbol of our family history. Later we made a genealogy book for both sides of the family, and we put that on the table, too. It has a picture of our daughters standing on a New England gravestone that takes us back thirteen generations. There is always plant life on the table to symbolize growth and life, a candle to symbolize warmth and closeness, and a goblet of wine for sharing.

"We hold up each symbol and talk about what it means. We look for examples of recent family events that helped us touch those feelings. And then," says Susan, "Gordon reads the words we wrote on the plane from England.

"The words out of context may sound corny, and they are private for us, a special sensitive ritual we don't share with anyone, even extended family members. It will mean much more," said Susan, "if families make up their own. The words should celebrate the family. They are an affirmation of our importance as a family.

"In discussing whether to share the words, we asked the children about changing them. They are very simple because the children were young then. The children were adamant against change. These words have almost a sacred quality for us."

The Toums' dinners have no set schedule. "Usually, we have three or four family dinners a year, on Christmas Eve, perhaps in June before the children scatter for summer trips, whenever an occasion or need presents itself. Sometimes we initiate a dinner; sometimes the children do."

Gordon Toum is a quiet, private man who takes pleasure in his work and family but has little need to talk about either with strangers. He needed the promise of anonymity to be comfortable discussing the dinners. As he talked, it became clear that they are powerful happenings. They have stood the test of time and have become a cherished means for celebrating how special it is to be a Toum.

No-Reason Parties

Sally and Richard Singleton have a different kind of dinner tradition, one geared to their young children. Although most parents spend a great deal of time on child-centered activities—sports, homework, weekend excursions—we use these times to teach lessons and deliver commercials. The Singletons' No-Reason Parties underscore the notion that some family times should be just for fun.

"Our children wished away their lives. As soon as their birthday party was finished, they began to plan for the next year, wishing the days in between would go quickly. It bothered us to see them missing the present. We decided our children needed special days more frequently, and they needed to know we all had the power to make any day we wanted special."

Sally Singleton is the mother of Joshua, Jeremy, and Jennifer, ages four, six, and eight, and the wife of Richard, a hardworking systems analyst who is outspokenly grateful that Sally cheerfully shoulders a disproportionate share of domestic responsibility.

"Two things we started then are established enough to qualify as traditions. We have a summer party every year, right around the time school is out. Each child invites several friends, and it is a big event. We have water-gun fights and games and cake and ice cream. I always have to assure other mothers it is not a birthday, so they won't send a present.

"At the same time, we started children's dinner parties. Our kids were miffed that they never got to go to the dinner parties we frequently have for our friends. For the kids, these meant pizza in the kitchen, a brief appearance in the living room, and bedtime without a story. So we started dinner parties for children, a couple of times a year, usually after we've had an adult dinner party and there are flowers on the table and leftovers in the kitchen.

"The kids get all dressed up and go out the back door. They come around to the front, and we usher them into the living room as guests. I set the table as I do for adults, serve a good dinner and a fancy dessert. The kids, in turn, are expected to match such civility.

"They love it. We do, too, because it is reassuring to see your children as guests. Has your child ever been out and the host family glowingly reported on his or her nice manners, leaving you delighted and mystified? Well, these dinners seem to bring out that best self."

✱

In an industrial world, family members no longer depend on each other for survival. Most of us go off each morning to separate lives. What ties a family together is our commitment to one another, our sense of caring and responsibility for each other.

By building traditions in ways that underline that commitment, that emphasize the importance of being a member of this family, we create a source of love and personal pride and belonging that makes living in a chaotic world easier. An anthropologist looking at our society writes: ". . . Our collective response to a demythologized, industrialized, technological environment is an escalating cycle of alienation, dissociation, and confusion." Family traditions counter that alienation and confusion. They help us define who we are; they provide something steady, reliable, and safe in a confusing world. They help us come together during difficult personal periods, like adolescence, when emotions make us angry. They help us keep in intimate contact until the crisis clouds have passed.

The Family Walk

Ann and Fred Lashing have a very simple but functional family tradition that grew out of their conscious recognition that they spent their days quite separately and needed to work at having family time.

Hero Lashing is the largest Lashing: an enormous shaggy dog. He lives with two Lashing adults, three children of assorted sizes, two gerbils, and forty-two fish. And he is the center of the Lashing family's best tradition: family walks.

Ann Lashing teaches school; Fred Lashing is a corporate executive who works on the wrong end of the morning rush hour. Ann says they are on "a morning schedule . . . If everybody is not in the kitchen before seven, we are running late. Two of us arrive cheerful and human. The other three are not built to function early. So we all read in the morning. You only talk at our breakfast table if it's an emergency.

"By 7:30 a.m., the fish are fed, the gerbils are burrowed in for their night, Hero is off having experiential education, and the rest of us are in cars, having barely communicated.

"We come together as a family at dinner, and after dinner, every night, regardless of the weather, we all walk Hero. Hero's time is our time to unwind, to catch up, to be together. We always walk twenty to thirty minutes. If you bicker or grumble or sulk—and, of course, it happens—you walk twenty paces behind, but you walk. The children understand that we parents need this time with them and that it is expected. Certainly, there are exceptions. Fred says 'we are inflexible but not rigid on this point.' The walking is healthy, it gives us a calm time away from telephones to unwind, and it gives each of us an appreciation for nature's changes. But the most important part is the talk time. We walk in all sorts of combinations and permutations. Sometimes we are a herd—but usually we are paired off, depending on who needs what at the time. Fred and I try not to use this time for our private communication but as time to talk with the children.

"We come home refreshed and ready to tackle our separate projects. It is hard to imagine our family without Hero," says Ann, "but impossible to imagine it without walking."

This notion of a special family time, firmly built into the family's schedule, can take many forms. One family goes out to dinner every Wednesday evening and takes the family kitchen calendar. This, says Ricki Davis, is Planning Night Out. The tradition has been adapted over the years. "Originally, when the kids were little, Paul and I went out to have a quiet time together. Then, as the kids got older, our lives got very splintered. Everybody had special needs, usually involving our only car, and we were not communicating well. So Wednesday night became a time for all of us to go out, away from the phone and the doorbell, with the calendar. We go to inexpensive fast-food places, but we sit and talk and get organized for the week. It is really important to us."

What, you might ask, is the difference between just going out to dinner and having a tradition? After all, lots of families eat out. It is attitude, activity, and regularity that shape traditions. Attitude says this is so important that all other things take lower priority. We don't plan important business meetings or trips, no matter how hectic our schedules, for the last Thursday in November, because we all know that is Thanksgiving. Activity gives structure. The Davises don't only eat, they bring their calendar and use the same planning process each week, and they always go on Wednesday, not Tuesday one week and Friday the next.

Kneading Time

A good example of taking something simple and elevating it to function as a new tradition is Alex Bardoff's bread baking.

When Alex Bardoff was a graduate student at the University of Washington, he lived in a large house with six other students. "Two of them were health-food zealots who badgered the rest of us to give up junk food for freshly baked cracked-wheat bread and vegetable soup. It was a pretty easy battle for them to win. Once you liberate your taste buds, they rebel if you don't keep treating them nicely. In my parents' house, men only went into the kitchen to empty the garbage. But I discovered I not only like eating good bread, I like baking it. It was terrific therapy after a day of microeconomics. As a bachelor, I impressed a lot of women by inviting them for a very cheap breakfast date of fresh fruit, homemade bread, and espresso."

Now happily married to another good cook, and father of four-year-old Lex, and ten pounds heavier, Alex Bardoff has made bread making a family tradition. "Saturday morning is almost always bread-baking time. Nina and Lex and I go to it, or if Nina needs escape time, Lex and I do it together. We try all sorts of things—croissants, raisin cinnamon pinwheels, herb breads—you name it, we have probably baked it. There is no greater pleasure for me than a rainy Saturday, dampening all other lures, good jazz on the stereo, coffee on the stove, Lex in his chin-to-ankle apron, Nina on a kitchen stool, and the 'yeastie beasties' at work . . .

"If I just think about baking when the mood strikes, I never get around to it. There is always something else to do on week-ends, errands to run, shutters to paint, bikes to fix. I found I'd start doing these things and time would get away from me and I'd never get to the bread. This way I do it first and I feel good all weekend. We are together as a family, calmly, happily. Sometimes Lex and I run errands while the bread is rising. More often, Nina and I just catch up on the week. The errands always wait."

Alex Bardoff found a way to take a private passion and turn it into a shared activity. He confesses to difficulty at first in having a cheerful toddler mess up his organized kitchen and disrupt his methodical ways. "Nina helped me see that bread baking was only one of the activities going on. Being together was just as important. Showing Lex patience and neatness and pleasure in work was part of what I was doing, too. Understanding all that, I stopped focusing on making perfect bread and started focusing on the process."

The Bardoffs' tradition was one of the few I collected in Seattle. I was excited about a chance to summer in Seattle in 1982 because I felt it would be an especially good place to collect new traditions. I imagined families far from relatives, using their beautiful setting as stimulus for imaginative new traditions. I thought there would be interesting cross-cultural mixes and lots of creative risk takers. I was wrong. It was harder to uncover traditions in Seattle than in St. Louis.

At first, I thought it was a problem of access, that I simply was not plugged into the community. One of the people I contacted was the minister of an established, urban Presbyterian church. He was not surprised by my observation. "We have found so many families that have trouble communicating. The outdoors becomes an escape and an excuse, not a vehicle for better communication. Families that do not start building good communication early run into trouble when their kids are teenagers, and they show up in my office wondering what went wrong." A woman who teaches a class for stepparents in the university extension program confirmed this. "This is not a particularly good place for traditions. People are focused on rugged individualism, on getting in touch with self. We see a lot of superficial relationships."

The Family Cup

Martha and Brett Kunkel have a family tradition that helps to establish positive communication. It is an especially good new tradition because there is a prop, an object anyone can easily acquire, that helps families get started.

Brett Kunkel is a Presbyterian minister. In his younger years, he spent some time doing graduate work in theology in California. He and Martha went off one sunny California weekend to a retreat on spirituality which had a table of handouts on ways to incorporate spirituality into everyday living. The idea of a family cup, a special goblet to toast special occasions, was described on one of these sheets.

The idea had appeal, and the Kunkels enlisted the help of a potter friend who obligingly turned out a large handsome pottery goblet. In the center he inscribed: "The Kunkels Celebrate Life."

"At first, we only used the cup for birthdays, Easter, and Christmas. We seldom drink alcohol, so putting wine in a goblet and toasting with it really did make us all feel festive and special. Gradually, we began to use the family cup to celebrate all sorts of family events," recounts Brett.

"We used it the last day our son was home before going off to college. We use it when good friends visit or when a child wins a special honor. We used it when I got my teaching job after ten years at home," says Martha, "and when Brett had his tenth anniversary with this congregation."

The cup is filled and passed from hand to hand for each

person to sip. Each toasts the celebrant by saying something loving about that person or offering a wish.

Martha and Brett have always loved the family cup, but Martha says there were times the kids would groan, "Oh, no, not the family cup again."

"Sometimes I felt it was something Brett and I foisted on the children, till the year Janie turned fourteen. We had a couple of scheduling conflicts that night and somehow never got around to getting out the family cup. At ten at night, I found Janie in her room sobbing. 'Nobody cares about me,' she wailed. 'We didn't even get out the family cup.'

"Of course, we immediately got out the cup. It's funny. I felt bad for her, but I felt good, too, that she cared and it was important to her. We toasted Janie that night for helping us to remember how important our family traditions are."

The "You Are Special" Plate

Laura and Dick Brand don't have a family goblet, but they have a similar tradition.

Laura Brand is a potter. She has a wheel and a small kiln in the basement, and in between the usual domestic trivia, she turns out enough solid work to do modestly well at local crafts fairs and Christmas bazaars. It was a surprise, then, when her mother-in-law's Christmas gift a few years back was a pottery dinner plate, a commercially produced one, glazed bright red, with the words "You Are Special Today" around the rim in white. "I thought it was a little hokey when I first saw it. It is not the kind of thing I would ever buy. But it was there, and somehow I started using it. We all have become quite fond of it."

It is reserved for important events, like birthdays. "When our son scored his first ice-hockey goal and when our daughter got accepted at a school she wanted to attend, we used it. I gave it to myself after a particularly successful crafts fair: the kids got it out for their father when he ran a particularly good race. And when my mother-in-law visits, we always set it at her place the first night she's here."

Laura's husband, Dick, elaborated on why he thought the plate was useful. "It is not enough to think family is important. We need to do things to support the family, to be vocal and direct about how important it is."

I had seen the same red plate at a neighborhood gift store where my children dissipate their allowances on bottle rockets and mini-dice and funny stickers. It had seemed awfully commercial, sitting there in its box—"hokey," as Laura said. After talking with the Brands, I went back and looked again. Seeing it through their eyes, I was tempted to buy it.

It doesn't have to be this plate, I thought; it could be an old china plate of Grandma's or one of those plastic plates that take children's drawings that you can make yourself. It can be a place mat or a cup, a crown or a sign. The plate is not what is important about the Brands' tradition. The key is the notion of having a concrete symbol to help recognize our special achievements and give an extra surge of warmth to our special days.

Once-a-Week Days

I was scheduled to talk with a parent-toddler group about traditions one morning. Conversation started slowly, reflecting my outsider status in a group of insiders. Then Sheila, mother of three, married twelve years to an electrical contractor, began talking quietly.

"I think tradition did my mother in. She had six children, and every holiday or birthday or family gathering was a major production. The turkey, fifty people, the Sears charge account. Before she passed on, she kept saying, 'If I can just make it to Bob's wedding (my brother) . . .' She did and was gone three days later, at fifty-two.

"And I repeated the same pattern for years. As a child, I had always had bad allergies and frequent trouble with breathing; this persisted into my adult life. I was told I would have to have surgery to correct a congenital breathing problem. As a Christian Scientist, for me that was not an option of choice. Two years ago, the week before Christmas, I ended up in a Christian Science sanatorium, barely able to breathe and totally exhausted.

"This may be hard to believe, but as I sat there depressed, it suddenly came to me that it was not my sole responsibility to mold this family into a cohesive unit and it was not my sole responsibility to make them happy. In that moment, my head cleared, my headache left, and I could breathe again. Since then, I have been able to breathe freely in a way I never could before.

"What I began to do was to use traditions to strengthen the weaknesses in our family. I don't like planning meals; that is a weakness of mine. And I felt the children needed more individual attention. So now, every week, every child has a day that is specially his, and Pete and I have ours. On your day, you make the choices you want. The kids pick the breakfast and dinner and that day they are excused from chores. Pete likes eggs goldenrod (hard-boiled egg whites creamed over toast, with the yolk sprinkled on top). It used to be a big deal to get around to making it; now that's his Sunday-morning breakfast, since Sunday is his day. If he wants to watch a game, we give it to him. I don't gripe anymore. But Saturday is my day. We eat out and the kids are not my responsibility unless I choose to have it so.

"We don't celebrate birthdays because I don't believe in recording age, but since the kids have a special day every week, there is ample opportunity for doing special things for them. We have been doing this for over two years now, and it really works for us."

"But what if a child wants blueberry French toast one morning and you only want to open a box of Cheerios?" I asked Sheila.

Sheila looked almost blank for a minute, as if the question did not make sense. "But I enjoy doing it because it is my business. It is my job. If I give the children choice in deciding what makes them happy, then it is not all my responsibility and that means a lot to me."

This kind of structure will not appeal to every family, but it works successfully for the Carpenters. In structure of her own choosing, Sheila has found freedom.

Traditions have always changed and adapted in response to cultural pressures. Since it is new situations that propel us to change, the more circumscribed and simple our lives, the fewer pushes to change. Primitive man had few external stimuli and he changed slowly. Our world presents us with regular difficulties that give us overdoses of stimulation. Advances in communications technology speed up the rate at which new ideas are absorbed in society; at the same time, new ideas are coming faster and from a wider arena.

In *The Shaman's Doorway*, anthropologist Stephen Larsen discussed our need for the myths associated with tradition. He intriguingly characterized his book as "a simple instruction manual for owning and operating a mythic imagination in the present time."

Serious historians have announced the end of an age, and our budding mythologies cry the beginning of a new—Aquarian—age, full of marvels and heralded by portents. What is certain is that our old mythological dynasties, the great orthodox traditions that have guided and shaped men's lives on this planet for thousands of years, have begun to release their hold on our collective imagination.

Some families have decided to reassert their hold on the past. Recognizing the stability of established tradition, they have reembraced parts of the past. My friend Becky, after years of trying to ignore a convent education, has renewed her Catholicism and uses its ritual to give her family a warm and rich pattern of tradition. People like Becky have astonished their families and sometimes themselves by picking up old, seemingly abandoned, threads and re-creating old traditions. In many American families where one or both parents come from a different culture, old traditions are imported to help children identify with this other culture. A Japanese woman married to a man from Peoria built a Japanese bath adjacent to her family room. It provides very special opportunities for intimacy and talk. A woman of Sephardic background has brought ladino music into her family celebrations. A Japanese woman has taught her daughter the rituals of the ancient tea ceremony.

But a return to the orthodoxy of the past is not the preferred path for most of us. Our grandparents led lives vastly different from ours. We may envy their sureness of what was right without sharing their beliefs. Still, looking backward is a good way to begin looking forward.

Psychoanalytic theory tells us our psyches are rooted in the past. Change that does not integrate the selves we keep secret as well as the ones we make public will be painful. If we cannot ignore our past, however, we are not condemned to repeat it. We can adapt it. The following traditions draw on the past. Four have religious overtones and one is focused on family history. They are small examples of how families have adapted very old traditional behaviors, like family prayer or Bible reading, to fit their present life-styles. In Sunday-Night Bible Reading, we see a family looking for a religious solution in the absence of religion. In Morning Circle, we find prayer, thankfulness, separate from an institutional affiliation.

Continuity with the past can be achieved by focusing on the intent of old traditions instead of on the rituals, and capturing that intent in new traditions.

Sunday-Night Bible Reading

Some of the things we most value as adults we do not relish as children. So it is with this tradition.

Ann and Paul Ragnole have different religious and cultural backgrounds. What they share and what attracted them to each other as students is a love of books and ideas. Their solution to differing religious upbringings is to avoid the issue—or at least to avoid distinguishing characteristics and to hone in on a common ingredient, the Bible.

"Our kids are familiar with our respective churches through their grandparents, but we have no formalized relationship with any organized religion and our children do not go to Sunday school. What we do instead is Sunday-night Bible reading. We have done this since our oldest could read," says Ann. "I felt the children should be familiar with the Bible, as much as a work of literature as a keystone of the church. We use both the Old and the New Testament and each week I pick out given passages, enough for five to ten minutes of reading. We are not particularly organized about the order of our reading. Some sections we have done many times; we do Ecclesiastes every year because the children like it; some sections we have yet to do. Everyone takes a turn at reading. The children regard this as a pain to be tolerated, but Paul and I made it clear a long time ago that we were going to do it, and we expected no complaints. Now the older ones are beginning to take pleasure in knowing the Bible when references to it come up in class or in books they are reading. Sometimes we will fall into a long family discussion from the reading; sometimes people vanish before the book is closed. We only insist the children stay for the reading. More frequently than family discussions, Paul and I will end up over cold coffee having our own conversations."

Other families might prefer reading tales of heroes and heroines, Greek myths, history, or poetry. For the Ragnoles, learning the Bible is a key part of this tradition. But equally important is the notion of sharing something meaningful over time, of growing familiar with and conversant in an area because it is a central part of family life. Children who are exposed to their parents' passions—but not forced to share them—are enriched as adults by that special exposure and frequently grow to love the subject themselves. Ten minutes a week may seem like a small dose, but in the end it provides a hundred hours of exposure without stretching small concentrations to the breaking point.

The Morning Circle

Melinda and Randy Pratter have three energetic towheads, the youngest of whom is about to go to nursery school and the oldest of whom is a standard ten-year-old: part little boy, part growing-up kid. Their mornings are typical: a few lost shoes, the crunch of cornflakes underfoot, the smell of coffee, and an aura of friendly chaos. Randy added a new ingredient, a special two minutes of quiet.

"This is Randy's tradition," says Melinda. "He is the one who always finds us before he leaves and brings us together. We gather in a circle and hold hands and one of the children, most frequently the youngest, says a little prayer. The older two coach him, making sure he includes their special thoughts. It's an extemporaneous prayer, and then we squeeze hands and kiss Randy goodbye.

"It is not a religious thing for us so much as a symbol of family unity, a coming together before we go off on our separate ways. We say a family grace in the same way, sitting at the dinner table.

"There are mornings when Randy is late and the family is irretrievably scattered on three floors. But for the past three years, I guess, we have managed to do it three or four mornings a week. It's just a Pratter thing."

I read of an interesting alternative for families who do not wish to say a religious grace at mealtimes. Consider a humanitarian grace that gives a tribute to acts of bravery and courage and deeds of kindness. A family might begin with one of the "graces" below and eventually write others of their own choosing.

> *Caring, sharing, being near*
> *Makes us each feel loved and dear.*

> *This family gives us pleasure.*
> *Love and caring is our treasure.*
> *We rejoice in our good fortune*
> *And hope others find their portion.*

As we gather for this meal, we take pleasure in our being together and pride in each other. Tonight we have special pride in . . . (the man who saved the six-year-old from drowning; the astronauts who left on their flight; Uncle John, who passed his exam; etc.).

When I was researching this book, I tried to find an appropriate place to raise the topic of new traditions in any conversation that lasted longer than ten minutes. One of my "commercials" for new traditions got tucked into a workshop I was doing for women employees of a state mental-health department.

Most of the women were on the lower and middle rungs of the career ladder, but the two most highly placed women in the department had also been invited, and it was difficult to structure the content to meet the wide range of needs. Still, I felt upset when, on the second morning, one of these senior women seemed more engrossed in writing than in participating.

At the coffee break, she materialized at my side and handed me several sheets of penciled copy. I grabbed a doughnut and slipped away to see what she'd written. The note began: "The subject of traditions fascinates me. I believe they provide an important sense of stability for all of us." She went on to write about why she felt tradition was important and how her family responded. One of the traditions she described was a generation tradition that not only strengthened the family but enriched the lives of others. Here is what she wrote.

Elder Evenings

"I come from a large, extended family—strongly based in tradition. My hometown was founded by my ancestors—the sixth generation is growing up there now. The large family gathering is central to social life. My brother is there and is doing a good job with his kids—they have a strong sense of their place in the generational flow. He has very deliberately done some things which I think have been good for them.

"When the kids were little—like seven and four—he started inviting one 'elder' at a time to dinner—a nice crystal and linen party—so the kids could meet and listen and ask questions of an elderly person who had lived there and made a contribution to the life of the community.

"When we are together, sitting around and talking, he often directs the conversation to our experiences and recollections of great-aunts and uncles, etc., long gone. One's siblings are likely to be the only validators of one's early childhood recollections, so it is good for us and it gives the kids a sense of our experience and the history and flow of our 'people.'

"He makes a big deal of replicating dinners from New England places—New Year's Day, he did the New Year's dinner from the Plymouth Plantation. We shared food none of us had ever eaten, like roast goose and parsnips braised in stout, and talked about what it must have been like.

"This sounds sort of cold and intellectual, but it is not at all. While we are verbal and cognitive, the experience is of sharing and appreciation of communality and differences—a comfortable feeling of who you are and where you fit in the grand scheme of life."

Car-Pool Wishes

This tradition is a prayer tradition for mutual support and encouragement slipped into a most unusual time frame.

I want to know Sheila Shelton Jones better. She is warm, candid, and thoughtful, and after a while, her straightforward looks melt into a special loveliness.

Sheila Shelton grew up in a black middle-class neighborhood in New Orleans. "I cannot," she says, "consciously remember interacting with whites all through my childhood, not until high school. Then I ended up the only black in my college class.

"I grew up with segregation, and the way we made it was

by being very close and helping one another. Then things began to move so fast. Educated blacks metamorphosed from invisibles to people with opportunity overnight. It had its price. In my own family there was great tension between those out of college, ready to take advantage of the times, who soared, and those younger members, left behind, still preparing, who suddenly lost their support system but had so much pressure on them.

"Things changed so fast that every three years there was a ten-year generation gap. The world opened up, but there was nobody out there to show us how to wend our way through. I yearned for family support then; and now, as my life is changing again, I still yearn for it."

Her favorite family tradition stems from this appreciation for a caring family. It is extraordinary to me because it slips into a time that is usually lost, car-pool time; it links a piece of the old black culture of church and prayer with a piece of the new, the private prep school.

My own morning car pools are uninspired. At worst, the sixth-graders taunt the fourth-grader, who in turn teases the first-grader. At best, people ride in groggy silence. In Sheila's car pool, her son and her best friend's son and daughter join hands to say the Lord's Prayer. Then each gives morning wishes, for self and for the other two children. The children are now in junior high and are full of wishes for how each day should be.

"I've tried to use this to teach the children imagination and expression as well as compassion. At first, they would just wish for a good day. I would tell them they had to use three positive adjectives or to name three things that would make it a good day or one thing they could do themselves to make it a good day.

"Issues come out in car-pool time now that might normally go unsaid, fears and hurts and yearnings. The children really support and bolster each other. This is something I imposed initially, but they recently showed its value to them. We have done this now for several years. This year, we had a chance to split up and each of us join another car pool. It would have meant less driving for me and less riding time for the children. I was pleased to find it was important to them to stay together and to keep our morning routine. I believe in its value enough to drive willingly five mornings."

Your Turn

The simplest thing can become a source of pride and pleasure for a family. This new tradition came from a woman who stood up shyly after I had spoken at a women's luncheon. "You know," she said, "how at family gatherings either nobody moves to help or everyone jumps up at once. I didn't like that. So I had the idea that I would put out name cards on the table and on the back of each card I would write a specific assignment: carve the turkey, clear the soup, organize the coffee. It works really well, and in our family it is a new tradition that everyone, not just a few women, help. It has eased a lot of holiday tension for me, and it makes me feel special."

Wishes for the World

Walk into Katie Conlan's dining room and you'll see a large, stark tree branch, silvery white and graceful, arching out of one corner. You might think, at first glance, that this was some interesting decorator's clever touch. And you would be wrong.

"This," says Katie proudly, "is the holiday bush. We hang something on it for every big occasion. For birthdays, we string up all the cards and bows; at Christmas, cards are fastened as they arrive. In February, of course, it's valentines, and pumpkins and ghosts in October. But we didn't have anything good for Thanksgiving.

"So we had a family powwow a few years back. The kids voted for chocolate turkeys; my husband and oldest son suggested we post the football-game odds. But in the end we decided to use our branch to make wishes for the world."

After Thanksgiving dinner, pencils and paper circles are brought to the table and everyone writes down his or her "wishes for the world." "Mostly it's serious stuff," says Katie, "but a five-year-old can be perfectly serious about wishing for lollipops for everyone in the universe.

"Some people may think it's foolish of us to write down 'I hope no more children die of hunger anywhere' and hang the circle on a tree branch. But we know our wishes don't cure hunger. They're just our way of remembering how much we have to give thanks for, and how hard we should be working to right the wrongs of the world."

The Best Thing in the Week

This last family tradition is special because it reflects what I hope this book is about. It came to us from friends who adapted it from their past, it is part of our lives, and it has gone on from us to other friends. It is free, simple to start, and a source of enormous pleasure for each of us.

Her maiden name is Goldstein. His family name is Donegal. They brought very different traditions to their marriage, and families that barely spoke to each other.

They were graduate students at the University of California when their first child was born, and they began worrying about what they wanted from family life.

Their first family tradition was borrowed from the Friday-night Sabbath service of Rebecca Goldstein's traditional Jewish upbringing. But Friday night was chosen as much for its appropriateness in their own academic week. In a Jewish Sabbath service, one lights and blesses the Sabbath candles and says prayers over the bread and the wine. These were cues to devising a new tradition that was comfortable for each of them.

Becky and Guy's Friday night meant "eating fancy." Eating fancy meant no toys on the table, but cloth napkins, candles, and a flower "borrowed from the landlord's garden." There was no dining room and no good dishes, and dinner could just as easily be leftovers as not, but they ate the leftovers graciously.

Becky tried to save Friday afternoons to bake bread with her son, and Guy made it a point to leave the library by 5 p.m.

The special part of the evening, however, the part our family has borrowed and that many friends have, in turn, borrowed from us, is sharing the best thing in the week. As the Donegals sat down to their candlelight dinner, accompanied by a cheerful infant's high-chair drumming, Becky and Guy told each other what the best thing in the week was. Even if it was an awful week, you had to come up with one good thing.

We, too, have incorporated telling the best thing in our week into Friday-night dinner. Our friends the Fullers borrowed the idea for Sunday lunch after church. Other friends now use it as part of their regular Sunday-morning telephone call to grandparents several states away.

We may forget sometimes to count our blessings, but we always remember to look for good things to share on Friday.

3

Religious Holidays

R ELIGIOUS HOLIDAYS should be the easiest to observe. They are the most likely to come with clear directions for established patterns and some customary activity. For me, they were the hardest, the times I felt most compelled to cook and most confused about what I wanted. Voices in my head kept whispering: "You should do this; you should do that." Some of us must contend with real voices phoning to tell us what we should do. All of us hear television voices that would have these holidays be retailed into our lives.

It took a long time for me to stop seeing these holidays as obligations and start seeing them as opportunities. These are times already bracketed out on our personal calendars, reminding us well in advance of an excuse to change the pace, gather the clan, or share with friends.

Realizing that holiday making is not a mother's private purview leads to the appealing notion that everyone should have a share in making a celebration. Young children can speak a few words, handle a simple task, or provide special decorations. Fathers can prepare a holiday food or plan a reading, a discussion, or a game. Guests and relatives should unhesitatingly be asked to be part of the family by contributing and participating.

When conventional religious traditions fit, observe them and preserve them. We need new traditions only when the old ones cease to serve, when they provoke unpleasant memories, migraine headaches, stomach cramps, or the petulance of a stubborn childhood. Or if the memories are so wonderful that we can never recapture them. Either way, this is impetus for experimentation and adaptation. I have a cousin who so hated his father's rigid observance of religious holidays that he refuses to set foot in a house of worship. Still, he cannot allow himself to work as usual on these days. Instead, he takes his whole family on long hikes to beautiful places. And I have a friend who loves Christmas so much and invests so much in her expectations that she is always disappointed.

Ask yourself: What is this holiday all about? What parts of it are most meaningful to me? What is the message I hope my children will absorb? Use old patterns but adapt them to your family's life-style and values, so these holidays can take on more meaning than ever before. Augment the joys and avoid the pains.

CHRISTMAS

December is a holiday month. It is a different month, a month with built-in opportunity for magic and memories, for time together to enjoy being a family. The work world slows, school calendars declare time out, and the endless surge of community activities and regular responsibilities stops in midstream to allow us time to celebrate. December offers us an opportunity. The trouble is that opportunity sometimes comes disguised in aggravation's clothing.

How many of us have Christmases to fit our visions? Our memories are of Christmases when we were children. We forget our parents were doing all the work. We want our children to have the same feelings, but we don't want to give up our own childhood fantasies.

We expect so much—of ourselves and of each other. In one day we try to do our best giving and our best being together and our best worshipping. We try to focus on our nuclear family and to reach out and make contact with those we love. Some of us try to reach out and include strangers who are alone. Some of us wonder about the worth of trying.

"My family wants us there for Christmas and my husband's family wants us with them, and the kids want to be home with their new toys. I start getting a tension headache before Christmas Eve, and it just sits there until it's all over and we have survived another year," says a young mother of three, who every December wishes for a desert island.

Paula says she is still working it out, too. "We used to go to my parents' house Christmas Eve and Ed's parents' house Christmas Day. Then I decided it would make more sense to have everyone come here, but about the only thing my mother and mother-in-law seem to agree on is that I don't make gravy correctly. We actually contemplated going to Barbados this Christmas as a way out, but that's no solution."

Yet Paula talks fondly of decorating the tree, of the ornaments from her childhood and those her own children have lovingly made over the years. "It's always fun to unwrap the ornaments and reminisce together. No matter how dreadful the children have been, they always seem delicious, even angelic, decorating the tree, padding around in pajamas and smiles."

Many Christmas traditions are well established: church and stockings and gifts, visiting grandparents and having in special friends. And it is impossible to talk about Christmas traditions without including food. Special dinners, favorite cookies, always-eaten pies are an important part of what people want to tell about their Christmases. But in choosing the Christmas traditions that begin this chapter, I was drawn to stories about changes, ways of celebrating that people said made Christmas a better, happier, more family time. I am sure there are many more wonderful "recipes" for new Christmas traditions and for other religious holidays to supplement these. Please share them on the form at the end of the book because people very much want to find ways to be responsible adults while rekindling pleasant childhood memories and replacing painful ones.

I like someone's notion of Thanksgiving being the introduction to December, to a month for good feelings, for sharing and caring and being together. For some, those feelings are helped by a slowing down, a reduction in the frantic pace December brings. The No-Surprise Christmas and No Shopping in December reflect these needs. Others of us relish the hustle-bustle, searching for a perfect gift amid jostling hordes, and midnight cookie baking. Whatever you do, Christmas is for your family. And it should be because you choose it to be, not because you feel culturally regulated or socially obligated to celebrate. Give yourself the gift of joy for December.

No-Surprise Christmas

"Christmas used to be marred by disappointment," says Terry Blum. "I'd search everywhere for just the right piece of train equipment, and then I'd pick the wrong thing. Our son would be disappointed and so would I. My husband, Tom, would take the children shopping and buy me an expensive silk robe. It was lovely, and I knew I was supposed to keep it and wear it, but can you imagine how painful it is to scramble eggs down the front of a $100 robe?

"We were all running around, especially me, searching for the perfect gift to please very picky people. All too frequently, the visions of the giver and the receiver didn't square."

Terry is a lecturer for Weight Watchers and is married to an airline pilot. They have a son, Tommy, thirteen, and a daughter, Samantha, eleven. Theirs is a busy, scheduled family with people going in different directions. For the Blums, the Christmas season has become a vehicle for drawing them away from individual pursuits, a coming together for good times to remember warmly. And it is now an event that is planned for all year, not just in a few hectic weeks in December.

"It is hard to realize I had so much trouble giving up our old way," says Terry, "but I worried about Christmas becoming another scheduled family project with assigned tasks, like cleaning the yard. I wanted it to be special and exciting. We are very rational people who, of necessity, have an organized and scheduled existence. I did not want to reduce Christmas to the level of ordinary, everyday activity, but I also did not want to keep on having frantic preparation for a morning of disappointment. We talked about it a lot and the kids had a lot to say. They were initially more enthusiastic about the changes than I was, so we decided to give it a try.

"We don't have surprises on Christmas anymore. We all shop for gifts together and we all plan what we are buying together. Our son tapes an envelope to the fridge and people stick notes in it all year, about great gift ideas for other people or for themselves. It is amazing how you can think of the perfect gift for Grandma in August and have lost it totally by November. This system is very informal. The notes get scribbled on paper towels or envelopes from the wastebasket, but at least they are written down.

"Thanksgiving weekend, we all sit down together, read the contents of the envelope, and discuss who wants what and what we need to give to whom. We don't start out with any set amount of money, but sometimes we will agree that there are too many expensive items and rethink in terms of cost.

"Then we plan shopping expeditions. Tom and Tommy may go off searching for train equipment, and Samantha and I will go clothes shopping, but we all go together to pick out my gifts and Tom's. We try to plan the shopping in conjunction with other things—a Christmas concert, dinner and a movie, a visit to friends. We are all so busy during the year that it is hard to schedule together-time doing things. The kids have sports and friends and school commitments. Tom travels and I work several evenings. Christmas is now a time when we make a conscious effort to curb outside commitments and to spend time doing things together as a family. The kids understand that this is part of their Christmas giving to us."

The presents are wrapped and put under the tree. Terry says there is still a newness to them on Christmas morning, even knowing what they are. "I always buy each person a book and Tom always buys each of us a silly gift, and we open these first so there is still a little surprise.

"This is going to sound strange to some people, but on Christmas Eve we pick up a super-deluxe pizza with everything on it and an ice-cream pie. I could spend all week cooking and not come up with anything the kids enjoy more. On Christmas Day, we have friends in for a really lovely lunch, which I can now handle because so many other burdens are gone.

"We have done this for four years now, ever since Samantha stopped believing in Santa Claus. It is one of the most liberating things that ever happened to me, and it really makes Christmas a celebration all December. Planning and shopping and being together in December is special for all of us, instead of being crammed all into one day."

No Shopping in December

Vivian and Alan Stone were also looking for a way to ease the pressures of Christmas. For some of us, the Christmas hustle-bustle is fun. Some people like being in the stores with avuncular Santa Clauses and tinny carols, but for lots of people, like the Stones, there is nothing fun about it. "I can't stand battling the traffic and the lines and the pressure," says Vivian. "Give me the August sales any day, when the stores are cool and uncrowded and the 90-degree parking lots are empty."

With this mind-set, the Stones have a firm Christmas tradition that says no shopping, except for food, after Thanksgiving.

"Thanksgiving inaugurates the Christmas season for us, and the Christmas season is a time for family and friends and baking and singing and being together. We do lots of entertaining and family things in December. The hard work is behind us.

"Because I only work part-time [as a nurse], it is easier for me to find time to shop than Alan, so I do most of it, but Alan and I do one or two evenings together because his input on some gifts helps. And Alan has a few gifts that he needs to do alone. We get a sitter for the kids, I meet him in town, and we make an evening of it. When we aren't feeling frantic, we actually can enjoy shopping together."

"But only occasionally," adds Alan.

Vivian wraps the gifts and hides them in the basement before Thanksgiving, along with the special purchases of jars of jam, bottles of wine, and tins of nuts. These can be used as last-minute gifts or eaten later.

This tradition was recounted at a dinner party one evening. I liked it because so many working families need to reduce the pressures of Christmas, but one of the other guests was skeptical. "It's a wonderful idea in theory," she said, "but impractical for all but the ultra-organized. We disorganized, spontaneous souls would procrastinate as usual."

"Ah," said Alan Stone, "if you just once experienced the feeling of freedom, you'd do it."

Some of us are permanently enamored of old traditions but plagued by finding time for them. In this next tradition, it isn't shopping that comes early but cooking.

So much celebrating involves food. At Christmastime, there is special emphasis on baking. Magazines are full of gorgeous recipes for cookies, stollens, Christmas candy, and special cakes and pies. Many of us have delicious memories of cutting the dough for cookies or spooning the fillings for Christmas pies and licking the bowl.

Lots of men and women said baking was an important holiday tradition for their families when they were children. Their mothers baked for eating, gifts, ornaments, and pleasure. Some of these daughters, and a few of the sons, now take great pleasure in holiday baking. It is one old tradition that cheerfully continues. But others have given up or continue out of obligation, not pleasure.

"I feel compelled to bake these damn cookies," said the personnel director of a large hospital. "I have gotten over having hot, perfectly balanced meals every single dinner. My mother would have died before she served tuna sandwiches and canned soup. I have no trouble with that, but I can't escape the cookies. It must give me pleasure at some level, but I am hard pressed to tell you where."

Operation Fruitcake

Sandra Kolwasky's fruitcakes are a tradition born of just such frustration. Sandy is an executive secretary to the president of a large corporation. She is married to a sales manager in the same company, and they have two daughters and lots of family nearby.

"I think having family close by is a terrific advantage for working parents. Holidays are easier because everybody chips in and cooks. Everybody in my family cooks and bakes and food is important. There is tremendous peer pressure on me to be a part of that. No one would ever say out loud I wasn't a good mother because I was too busy working to bake, but they would believe it, and I guess a part of me still believes it, too. And I enjoy cooking. I am a good cook, and when there is time, baking is a great tension releaser.

"But the Christmas season is so hectic. My boss doesn't slow down for the holidays, and my job is pressured normally. In December there is a lot of socializing because of my husband's job in sales, and no matter how organized we try to be about presents, there is always last-minute shopping and wrapping. It is the time of year when I have the fewest hours for the kitchen. Baking isn't therapeutic then, it's one more job to squeeze in. Yet it is important to me to have homemade baked goods to give to neighbors and friends as well as relatives.

"Fruitcakes are my perfect solution. As soon as it gets chilly, sometime in November, it's fruitcake time. All of us give over two weekends to stir up a billion fruitcakes. Everybody chops or shells or peels or stirs. We make different kinds and different sizes and we like to experiment with at least one new recipe. Then we wrap them in brandy- or rum-soaked cheesecloth and put them away.

"It's done before Thanksgiving. I have something homemade to keep my guilt at bay and to maintain my domestic status. I have wonderful small gifts, especially those last-minute gifts you need quickly, and it's really fun to do. Then the kids and I can bake cookies or not as the mood strikes us near Christmas. We like to try new recipes, and if they are terrible, it doesn't matter. Or if we never get around to it, that doesn't matter either."

These next five Christmas traditions speak to the day of Christmas and to ways to make it worthy of all the advance publicity. Although each is focused on Christmas, think about adapting the ideas to other religious holidays. Homemade decorations are fun for any celebration; homemade services fit any event.

A Personal Christmas Tree

Cynthia Nesbitt is a tall, solidly built woman who is wearing a jogging suit and has specks of blue paint on her arms. As we have coffee in her large sunny kitchen, she comfortably declares, "I am a housewife who hates housewifery. My house is not very clean, and I am not a very good cook. I'd rather eat yogurt standing up at the kitchen sink, and if I did not have four kids who are usually hungry, I'd probably never cook anything fancier than toast."

Cynthia compensates for these dispassions by being a splendidly cheerful mother, an energetic hiker and camper, and a gifted do-it-yourselfer. And she directs all this energy each year toward Christmas. "I love Christmas. It has everything a family needs . . ."

The Nesbitts have a personal Christmas-tree tradition that echoes a tradition I heard about in one form or another from many other families, but Cynthia Nesbitt is a purist in execution.

The Nesbitt tree is decorated entirely with handmade, homemade ornaments. Some are gifts from friends, but most are the work of Cynthia and her family. The usual colored balls are replaced by dozens of small round or oval frames, fashioned from cookie dough, fabric scraps, or macramé, fitted with small pictures of the children at every age. There are shiny origami birds and glittery silver chains recycled from chewing-gum wrappers. There are patchwork balls and stained-glass angels and straw stars and green and red blown eggs, all done with varying levels of competence.

"The children and I make new ornaments each year and save the best after Christmas for the 'in-perpetuity' boxes. Each child has his own box, his own collection of ornaments, which one day go with him to his own family. We make ornaments all year, whenever the mood strikes. It is a great thing to do on gloomy days or really hot days, much better than television. We use stuff from family vacations, seashells and rock crystals and dried flowers. The ornaments are a family chronicle. I can't imagine buying stuff, no matter how pretty, when there is so much fun in hanging your own family history on the tree."

I told a friend about the Nesbitts' tree and she was reminded of a marvelous incident in her childhood. One Christmas she and her sister decided that the family tree should be a more personal, hand-decorated affair. Their two brothers were horrified. The Christmas tree had always, but always, been decorated with the same red bows and silver stars. If one could change the tree, one might change all the order of childhood. Her brothers could not articulate such an abstract concept, but they were fierce in protecting established family patterns. "My parents were very wise," my friend said. "We simply had two trees that year."

Children like repetition. It helps to establish family identity, and it is comforting when, especially during the teen years, the world seems topsy-turvy.

All-Day Christmas

One evening a couple of teenagers described to me how they thought Christmas Day should be. After all the preparation, the kick ought to last at least the whole day.

Betsy O'Connor is fourteen going on fifteen. She's a city kid, an endearing mix of poise and sophistication and giggly vulner-ability. Betsy, her older sister, Ann, who is just graduating from high school, their parents, and a friend of Ann's talked to me about family traditions one night over a Betsy-made chocolate-fudge cake.

We started talking about Christmas, about what the girls will remember when they are grown, what they will tell their children about Christmas.

"I always considered our holidays better than everyone else's," confessed Betsy. "I thought I was luckier than my friends because our Christmas lasts all day. I looked down on the kids who got up at seven and had it all over by eight."

An O'Connor Christmas Day begins slowly. "We don't open presents until our parents are up, and you have to wait until they wake up themselves. Then we do our stockings, which are up-stairs. After that, we all troop into the kitchen to make cocoa and cinnamon toast and scrambled eggs. Everybody dashes past the living room and does not look, so the gifts will be a complete surprise.

"One year," said Ann, "I caught sight of something big and red. It upset me all through breakfast just knowing that much, because it really is family tradition to let the suspense build and not look at all. None of us ever looks. Not knowing is part of the excitement of Christmas.

"Finally, we all go into the living room and open presents one by one. Then it's time to get out all the stuff for Christmas dinner. We get out the silverware and the linens and the good dishes, and we all help set the table and get dinner started. I guess we could take it out the day before, but that is as much a part of Christmas as anything.

"Then we get all dressed up. Usually we get new clothes for Christmas and we try to wear all our new things. By that time, the dinner company starts arriving and there are more presents.

We eat and we make toasts and we sing. Afterward, there are charades.

"I like it because the whole day is Christmas, the whole day feels warm and family," sums up Betsy.

She has spoken an O'Connor truth. Everyone agrees, including the adults, who, with a reasonable night's sleep and a pot of coffee before the onslaught of presents and children who think helping is fun, find Christmas a good day, too.

Other families described other ways of making Christmas an all-day event. Some go to Grandma's for Christmas dinner, some have family in for brunch. Some go to church before presents and others go after. What people value, it seems, is a comfortable pattern that gives definition to the entire day.

Savoring the Season

One family decided a day was simply too short. Julio and Estelle Rigaldo hurry through the weeks, juggling jobs and children, chores, church activities, and family. Their hectic schedules don't give them much time to savor happy moments.

"I'm used to being busy," says Estelle. "But our holidays had the same frantic feeling as the rest of the year, and we decided to change it. We started with the kids' presents. It would never occur to us to serve them a whole year's ice cream at one sitting, yet we were doing the equivalent—letting them rip through practically a year's worth of presents in an hour. We felt we were encouraging greediness—and no joy, no wonderment could come from that."

The Rigaldos called a halt to Christmas-morning madness by

declaring a new tradition. Now gift-getting is spread from Christmas morning to New Year's Day. "The kids don't forget about their other presents," says Julio. "In fact, they'll rattle and poke the boxes a couple of times a day. But this system puts their gifts in better perspective. And they appreciate the gifts more. A small thing that might have been tossed aside if it were opened Christmas morning is a treat when it comes all by itself four days later. The children get much more pleasure from this process, and so do we."

Happy Birthday, Jesus

Mary Jane Wallace is one of those amazing and unconsciously intimidating women who come pretty close to doing it all. She is the head of a good and growing private school, a job that has endless meetings, constant crises, and one hundred and fifty families who expect her to know them and their problems well. She is involved in her church and her community. She and Richard have three children, eight, ten, and fourteen, who are wholesome and cheerful and do well in school. They sing in choruses, play violins, run track, and do all the usual things that require being chauffeured hither and thither. The Wallaces have no household help, but, at least on the days I have been there, the house is neat. And come holidays, Mary Jane is a whirlwind of domestic energy, baking, cooking, and orchestrating. I said Christmas and she said, "Cookies, dozens and dozens of cookies." I used to think such energy was the result of organization. Now I think it's all metabolism, so I don't feel bad anymore, but still, it is impressive.

The Wallace Christmases are very traditional, filled with food and family and church and presents. "Yes, it's hectic, and yes, it's busy, but no, not stressful," say Mary Jane and Richard. "It's fun. It's Christmas. It wouldn't feel right not to do all those things. We do all the things we did as children and some things of our own that we've added over the years."

One of those additions is the Christmas cake. The day before Christmas, Mary Jane and the children bake a big cake and the children specially decorate it, planning something different each year. This is Jesus' birthday cake. It is Christmas dinner dessert. When the cake is served, everyone sings "Happy Birthday" to Jesus. "It is a joyous way of remembering what Christmas is really all about."

The Family Service

Theresa McNeil grew up going to Midnight Mass and coming home to a big family breakfast. It was a tradition she loved and continued as an adult. But when she became the parent of four children, the tradition became a trauma. "Getting everyone dressed and organized, keeping them awake or still, and dealing with their exhaustion Christmas Day drained the pleasure.

"One year I just said, 'I have had it.' I am not going to do this to Kirk and me or to the kids one more year. We are not going to Midnight Mass. We are going to have church right here, in our own living room. And we did. We wrote our own service. Everybody got into pajamas, and we lit lots of candles and we all took part. We had our service at 10 p.m., breakfast at 10:30, and wonder of wonders, Kirk and I almost made it to bed by midnight. It was wonderful. The kids loved it, we loved it, and we have done it ever since. All the kids are certainly old enough to go to church now, but we would not dream of giving up the most meaningful part of Christmas."

HANUKKAH

Because Hanukkah falls in close calendar proximity to Christmas, it is influenced by Christmas traditions.

Hanukkah would be a minor Jewish holiday if it came in another month. The holiday celebrates freedom from religious tyranny and the rededication of the Temple of Jerusalem. The modern symbol of Hanukkah, the eight-branched candelabrum called a menorah, was a late adaptation. Even later, in response to the dominant Christian culture, the tradition of gift giving was incorporated in the Hanukkah celebration.

Christmas and Hanukkah are not the same, but children are given to compare them. It is hard for many Jewish families to resist the pull of Christmas customs and to decide on their own approach to Hanukkah.

The Hanukkah Plan

This Hanukkah tradition is my own, a cherished Lieberman tradition. It has given me some of my warmest, most endearing, family-proud moments.

The tradition was triggered by rising dissatisfaction with how we spent the December holiday period, a period in which I had unwittingly confused consumption and celebration. It was shaped in discussion with our children, who first wrote it down, since we had to wait a year to implement our design.

What they wrote was our formula for the eight nights of Hanukkah.

Religious Holidays

1st night:	Big-Gift Night
2nd night:	Mommy Night
3rd night:	Daddy Night
4th night:	Poem Night
5th night:	Small-Gift Night
6th night:	Gift-of-Self Night
7th night:	Giving Night
8th night:	Word Night

As it turned out, the order was not immutable. It is adjusted to fit each year's schedule. And, in truth, the eighth night originally read Sweets Night. At the last minute, I declared us overcaloried, and searching for a substitution, we took inspiration from the Hanukkah song that says, "And the word broke their swords." Otherwise, the grand scheme remains unchanged.

We parents are responsible for Big-Gift and Small-Gift Nights. The children are responsible for Mommy and Daddy Nights, and we all contribute to the remaining four.

Our first Poem Night is a burnished memory for me. The theme is always family. Michael set the tone. My perfectionist husband worked on his poem for weeks, in airplanes, in lonely motel rooms. I finally closeted myself in the bedroom one Sunday afternoon and suddenly had a proliferation of mediocre metaphors to sort. Seeing us struggle and listening to us laugh and moan about our efforts inspired the children. On Poem Night, each read his poem by the fire, puffed with pride in himself and in the others.

Gift-of-Self Night requires a gift of ourselves to another family member or the whole family. It has to be more than an extra hug but not something so hard one cannot deliver (like a clean kid's room). Our son Jonathan, for example, gave extra reading time for several weeks. Michael gave the children no nagging about table manners for the entire school vacation.

Giving Night focuses outwardly. Each child must give a sum of his own money, to be matched by us, to a charity of his choice. We do the same. There is much discussion that night about how much each child will give and to what place his precious funds, and ours, should go. A giving gift need not, of course, be money.

For Word Night, each of us finds a word he thinks will stump the others. We all guess at the meaning, seriously and most unseriously.

Our new Hanukkah design gave us a wonderful family week that did not depend on cooking and was not my sole responsibility to orchestrate. It made us feel good about ourselves and each other.

Light a New Menorah

The Jewish holiday of Hanukkah is also known as the Festival of Lights. On each of eight nights, families light one candle of the menorah—the traditional candelabrum—until all eight glow to symbolize religious freedom. In Sara and Allan Grossman's home the glow is particularly bright, since the Grossmans have not one menorah but eleven.

"When the children were little, they would always fight over who would light the first candle," explains Sara. "We solved the problem by giving each child his own menorah. At first they were just 98-cent tin jobs. Then, when Jonathan was in third grade, he made a lovely menorah in wood shop. David wanted to upgrade, too; he'd seen a ceramic one that he liked, so we bought it for him. Allan and I had always used a slightly skewed old brass one from his side of the family—his dowry, Allan says. So we had three menorahs for four people, and that's how it began.

"Now we still have four people but eleven menorahs. Each year we add a new one. We're all involved in choosing it, and the new one is the first lit each year. In the light of nearly a hundred candles the values of Hanukkah are glowingly illuminated."

EASTER

I nominate Easter egg dyeing as the best-loved national custom. Whenever I asked young people about their favorite family traditions, Easter eggs showed up. More than one parent talked about college students who still insist on Easter egg hunts. I am not absolutely sure, but I think every family I interviewed had some Easter egg or Easter hunt tradition. The first of the following two Easter traditions is the most original form of hunt that I found. The second is interesting because it preserves eggs from year to year, giving them some of the nostalgia we also get from Christmas ornaments. You will find a third Easter tradition having to do with Lent in Chapter 10, "Giving Traditions."

The Easter Nickel Hunt

This is a neighborhood Easter hunt that older kids don't outgrow.

Harold Fleigelmeyer would make a wonderful department-store Santa Claus. He is sparkly, jovial, and corpulent. All the kids in the neighborhood know Harold, and more impressive, he knows most of them.

"I am a people person. I like knowing my neighbors. I want a sense of community. Our first house was in a ticky-tack box that looked just like all the other boxes on the street. And each box burst with little kids who spilled over onto the lawn and the street and the neighborhood playground, parents in tow. We knew the kids because of our kids, and as a result we got to know their parents and it was a nice place to live.

"We outgrew the house. My law practice was going well, and it was time to move. Phyllis and I fell in love with this house [a large English Tudor on almost an acre], but it is a very different neighborhood. I felt the need to create a little community action and that's how the Easter hunt got started. Now it is my claim to fame in the eighteen-and-under set.

"The first year I got $20 worth of pennies, and I got my kids to put handbills in all the neighbors' mailboxes announcing the Fleigelmeyer First Annual Easter Penny Hunt, open to all under the age of eighteen anytime between 10 a.m. and 2 p.m., fifteen minutes of hunting per person.

"We must have had a dozen kids show up plus ours, and it was fun. Trouble is, I worried about the pennies they didn't find that would cause a problem for the lawn mower, so I went back to candy. Each piece is now worth a nickel. I discovered as the kids got older a penny wasn't enough incentive. I scatter five hundred jelly beans around the grounds and put up $25 in nickels. Even a twelve-year-old will hunt, for the possibility of making a quick buck. My golf buddies think I'm nuts, letting all those kids trample the lawn, but you know what, the grass grows anyway and the kids are pretty careful and everybody has fun. The kids come and sometimes their parents wander down, too, and I indulge my street-kid proclivities."

Egg Ornaments

Here is a way to build an Easter tradition by preserving special dyed eggs.

Anya Gunderson Thomas looks European. She is tall and deliciously thin, with angular bones in all the right places. She shops in the same humdrum places I do, but she always looks distinctively chic, as if she were wearing next year's designer sports clothes.

She is a microbiologist with a Ph.D. and is married to one of her former professors. They worked in the lab together for several years before she chucked science to have a baby and let her considerable artistic talents out of the closet.

Anya bakes wonderful herb breads and makes heavenly cold vegetable purees; she arranges flowers with the eye and the instinct of a Japanese master; she weaves beautiful, feathery, woolen shawls and is developing impressive skills in her first love, pottery.

None of these awesome talents has impressed my eight-year-old son, who spends considerable time playing army in the Thomases' back yard. But when Anya brought out the Thomas egg collection for Easter, our son was profoundly moved. He was, in fact, mesmerized.

The eggs are done in the Eastern Orthodox tradition and have intricate and colorful designs, enameled through a process of waxing and dyeing and painting. Many of them are blown out and are fragile, jewel-like creations. It was these that Seth found especially enchanting.

But also with the blown eggs are the family eggs that Bryan Thomas, Seth's compatriot, has made each year. These dyed eggs were not blown and so are not fragile. They are hard and a pellet rattles within. They show Bryan's progressive talent through the years and are charming.

Anya and Bryan begin with a raw egg, clean it with vinegar, put on a design with liquid wax, and dye it first in yellow as a background. Then Bryan works on his designs and dyes. Eventually, the wax is melted off slowly in the oven and the egg is varnished. Anya just uses clear nail polish. The varnish keeps the egg from smelling, and within a year the insides petrify and it is hard as a rock.

In this way, Bryan's eggs are kept from year to year, like Christmas ornaments. The eggs are displayed in abandoned bird nests that Anya and Bryan and cooperative friends have found, to dazzle and enchant both adults and eight-year-olds alike.

When Anya promised to show Seth and me how to make these eggs, Seth nearly burst with excitement. Bryan felt pretty important, too.

PASSOVER

This next new tradition is for the Jewish holiday of Passover, celebrated with a seder, the meal portrayed in Leonardo da Vinci's painting *The Last Supper*. It is another of those traditions so easily transferable to other holidays and so helpful in giving the holidays meaning for children.

The Passover Play

Traditional Jewish Passover seders are long. Before you can eat the source of the tantalizing smells, you have to read pages and pages from the Haggadah. The length of the reading usually correlates with one's orthodoxy.

Jacob Harriman remembers vividly his grandfather's interminable seders. "In order to get through it, the adults read so quickly you could not understand the words even if you were paying attention. I hated it. I vowed I would never do the same for my children."

The Harriman Passover seder is, instead, a play that unfolds the Passover story. The children are coached in the plot and assigned characters, as are invited guests. There is no set script.

Each person speaks lines of his own invention, but Rachel Harriman holds a few children's rehearsals beforehand to warm up. The plot never changes, but the play is the essence of living theater. As the children grow and understand more or focus their interest on different parts of the story, the play changes from year to year.

Someone must represent those who want to leave Egypt; someone plays the timid Jew who fears life in the desert; someone is a rebel; and someone is a diplomat. Someone is Moses, and someone is the Pharaoh's representative. "It is a community meeting," Jacob announces, "and we are discussing what we are to do. Let the play begin . . ."

"My grandfather," says Jacob, "is probably roaring in his grave, but in my own way I am true to his spirit. He had a great love for Judaism, an inquiring mind, and a fondness for storytelling. Our Passover play, far better than his seders, passes on these qualities."

4

Birthdays, Anniversaries, and Other Rites of Passage

THE SPOTLIGHT is on us! Rites of passage are moments that are especially ours. They mark our progress. Change and growth cannot, of course, be encapsulated in a single day, but these formal events give symbolic representation to our moving forward.

In theory, it might make more sense to celebrate middles than beginnings or ends. Maybe graduation or a fortieth birthday is not the truly meaningful moment. It might be a day in May when it hits you that your spouse is really a spectacular person or that you suddenly don't need to fight with your mother anymore or that your teenager has become a together, sensible human being. These "Aha!" moments are truly the important rites of passage, but they are too ad hoc for celebration or ceremony. And sometimes they are too private to be made the center of family sharing.

Edwin Friedman, a Washington, D.C., family therapist, believes the times before and after major rites are important moments in restructuring family relationships. The ceremony is not the passage, he notes in *The Family Cycle: A Framework for Family Therapy*, but it is an opportunity to lessen tensions and facilitate bonding.

Ceremonies celebrate. From an emotional systems point of view, they are not in themselves efficacious . . . On the other hand . . . the celebration event itself can be a very useful occasion for meeting people, for putting people together, for reestablishing relationships, for learning about the family (both by observation and the hearing of tales), for creating transitions, for example, in leadership, or for the opportunity to function outside or against one's normal role, e.g., getting "looped" when one has always been expected to be the sober one.

The commonly recognized "big moments" become the occasions that bring us together to give praise or comfort or sustenance to each other. These events, like religious and national holidays, carve a space in our busy lives to focus on the family unit and on each individual within it.

What I love most about my husband is that he simply loves me, regardless. Whether I achieve great things or accomplish prodigious feats, whether I pick up the cleaning or listen cheerfully, I can still count on being loved. That does not happen very many places in the world, and it is comforting beyond description. I suppose every day should be a celebration of this, but, mainly, every day is hectic. Anniversaries and birthdays and Father's Day remind me, nudge me, to take time to focus on my good fortune. Instead of shouting "Love you" as I race out the door, I am guided to write a love letter, to offer a toast in front of my children, to hunt down a special gift, to set aside time that says "You are special" and "We are special."

These special days are also a way of sharing responsibility for caring about the family. Children can be as responsible for planning a birthday celebration as parents. If our children are partners in planning, it will help them to establish an overriding tradition of caring as adults.

If religious and national holidays bring extended families

together, rites of passage strengthen the bonds of friendship and help us keep in touch with people we care about but may seldom see. Crowded calendars that never mesh somehow manage to coordinate for special birthdays. Logical restraints against lengthy long-distance phone calls get put aside to offer congratulations.

There is another advantage to establishing tradition for rites of passage. As much as these days can make us feel special, they can be setups for disappointment. When you were young, do you remember eagerly looking forward to something and planning in your mind just how it would be? Then it happened, but not according to plan. You were disappointed. Tradition can protect against disappointment. Instead of hoping people will guess our wishes or carry out our dreams, we can anticipate the expected. We can even help plan and execute the family traditions so they will match our expectations.

Holidays like Christmas or Thanksgiving frequently bring expectations from others. Parents and in-laws and aunts and uncles and brothers and sisters all have needs and wishes about our proper role in celebrating. Birthdays, anniversaries, graduations, awards, engagements, and the like are ours. We can exercise our own preferences more easily. These may be better times around which to build very special family celebrations than the larger holidays, which demand so much sharing from us.

It is a tricky issue—when to assert one's preferences and when to yield to those we love. By the time I married, I had suffered through eleven weddings of roommates or close friends, suffered because in every case there had been conflict and dissension between the bride or groom and her or his family. Dr. Bernard Klionsky, one of my husband's professors, gave us good advice: The marriage is for you, but the wedding is for your parents. When balloons and cheesecake wedding cake were vetoed, I gracefully retreated, powered by the memories of all those other wedding conflicts. I cannot say when to insist and when to retreat; the balance is different for each of us. However, religious and national holidays may be the best occasions for compromise, and rites of passage our times for self-indulgence.

There are many ways of using the opportunities rites of passage provide. In my fantasy world, they are excuses for making some days larger than life. Imagine being awakened the day of high-school graduation by the high-school marching band on your front lawn, or celebrating your twenty-first birthday with fireworks. I fantasize a medieval festival on my fortieth birthday to honor the Middle Ages (mine).

These spectacles have great appeal to my Cecil B. De Mille mentality. I am superb at dreaming them up while waiting in a school car-pool line, but they are seldom consistent with my financial or emotional resources. I can hardly manage time to buy a simple present at the local discount store, let alone stage an extravaganza. And, unfortunately, the old adage is mostly wrong. It is not just the thought that counts. It is also the deed! Many of the traditions in the following sections seem to work precisely because they are not extravagant. They are manageable for busy, working families, and they are meaningful to the people involved.

This chapter concentrates on passages of time. Omitted are loss and inclusion rituals like those associated with marriage, birth, and death, which require a more complex treatment. The focus is on birthdays and anniversaries, those repetitious events that lend themselves to establishing tradition, and a tradition each for confirmation, graduation, and bar mitzvah, which, along with getting the car keys, symbolize puberty rites in our society.

BIRTHDAYS

I spoke earlier about the natural longing for stability in an age of great instability. If the world around is chaotic and sometimes

incomprehensible, then the family is an oasis, an anchor of re-
liability and loyalty, a place where we are important because we
are there. Birthdays give us a day that is especially ours, a chance
to take an ordinary day and make it larger.

Small things done year after year seem especially valuable
for birthdays. The mother of a child entering adolescence said,
"David's birthday seems to be the only time he will allow himself
the comfort of childhood now. I was surprised at how upset he
got when I suggested a different kind of cake this year." The
widowed father of a ten-year-old spoke warmly of the annual
father-son canoe trip he gives himself each birthday, and a world-
wise seventeen-year-old proudly displayed the silver dollars he
has collected from his grandfather on each birthday.

Birthday traditions are a lovely way to feel important. But
what happens when our day comes and no one is around to
celebrate? Coupon Birthdays and Summer-Winter Birthdays are
two solutions.

Coupon Birthdays

Arthur Mason is a successful Wall Street lawyer who does lots of
litigation work. When he is in the middle of a court case, he is
a bear. He growls when approached and needs lots of hibernation
time. His wife, Kirsten, is a television producer and travels frequently. Her job sounds glamorous but much of the time is just
grueling.

Arthur and Kirsten were in their mid-thirties when they had
their child, Jennifer. Jennifer, now seven, is testimony to the fact
that two working parents can raise a happy, cuddly, self-assured
young lady. But Arthur and Kirsten think about their family needs
as seriously as they do their work needs.

When Kirsten was in France for Jennifer's first birthday and

Arthur was in New Orleans for her second, it became clear that rigidly scheduled celebrations were setups for disappointment. On the plane from New Orleans, Arthur invented coupon birthdays.

On Jennifer's birthday, there is an envelope waiting. In it is the first of three easy clues that lead to the coupon envelope. The coupon envelope always has a cake and ice-cream coupon, a gift coupon, and a party coupon. Last year, it had three "breakfast with Dad" coupons and one "staying up late at a dinner party" coupon and one "out to lunch with Mom and a friend" coupon. The coupons have silly poems and funny pictures and "I Love You" around the borders.

Jennifer, Arthur, and Kirsten schedule the cash-in times together. It must sound strange to some families to have to negotiate a time for cake and ice cream, but it seemed less strange to Jennifer's parents than having a disappointed little girl whose birthdays came when parties were not possible.

Once a time is scheduled, says Arthur, "I treat it as I would a date with a very important client. If something tempts me to break it, I ask myself, 'Would I cancel Mr. Such-and-Such?' If the answer is no, Jennifer's got her date. I look forward to our times together. If I'm traveling a lot, we might even go out to breakfast together on a school morning. I figure our relationship is at least as important as arithmetic."

For Jennifer, planning how to cash a coupon is part of the fun. There is pleasure in savoring all the possibilities and looking forward to the event. Because her parents take the coupons so seriously, Jennifer feels important. She boasts to her friends that her birthdays go on and on.

Summer-Winter Birthdays

This is a sensible way to avoid having a birthday party when no guests are around to come.

When Jason Springsteen, age eleven and a half, told me his birthday tradition, I wanted to hug his mother. Unless you, too, had years of August birthdays when no one was home for your party, you cannot appreciate how deprived a child with an August birthday can feel.

My birthday is August 11 and Jason's is August 21, perfectly dreadful times to have birthdays, especially if you like lots of presents.

Probably the best tradition is not to make babies in November; wait a month. Make babies in December for the holidays; then they can celebrate in September, which is a wonderful month to have a birthday. However, since no one anywhere evidences any interest in this tradition and babies continue to be born all through July and August, parents should know about the Springsteen solution.

Jason's really important birthday is his half birthday. August 21 is just a way station, marked by some cake. No presents. No cards. Even grandparents cooperate. February 21 is Jason's official celebration date.

This, Jason explains, is lots better than having your party early or late, " 'cuz that way you don't really have any special day. You have to wait if you want to do it in September, and if you do it in July, some guys are at camp, and if you have it before school is out, you feel stupid when kids ask when your birthday really is.

"Besides, this way I get a cake and a half." To note the unusualness of Jason's way of celebrating, his mom makes two cakes. One is a whole cake, which this year had eleven candles and one for good measure, and one is half a cake, which has one candle, half for a half year, half for good measure. The second half is frozen, and that is what is retrieved on August 21.

For those of you with birthdays in October or May, this may seem silly. But take my word for it, this is creative child psychology. Having an August birthday can give a kid a real sense of deprivation. I know.

Only-Me Birthday Dinners

Some kids have an opposite problem. It is not the absence of people; it is too many people horning in on the action. Only-Me Birthday Dinners is just the tradition then. A birthday dinner out is a gift of uninterrupted attention from both parents simultaneously.

"This house is a zoo!" says Carrie Harriman. I know her house well. She lives nearby and her oldest and my oldest are friends. She has three boys, five, seven, and ten. Like their father, they are big (the ten-year-old threatens to dwarf my own 5′ 2″ very soon), athletic, and competitive. And they are noisy. They are nice, polite kids, but, like puppy dogs, always squiggling and jostling and rolling with one another. And they are always hungry. Her house *is* a zoo.

But that is not Carrie's worst problem. Her worst is car pools. With swimming, ice hockey, basketball, baseball, soccer, tennis, gymnastics, and no two practices ever at the same place at the same time, Carrie feels like a human station wagon.

Her second worst problem is giving each boy his own space, his own individuality in a fast-paced, noisy, competitive environment. Carrie and Dick Harriman work on this in many ways. Their birthday tradition is one small but important piece of this conscious effort to deal with each son individually.

"Each boy, for his birthday, chooses his favorite restaurant, and Dick and I take him to dinner—alone. We get a sitter for the other two. This is just his special time. The first time we took our middle son out, we were astounded. Once he got started talking, he could not stop. It hit us how seldom he gets to talk with no one interrupting him.

"Our youngest son still thinks McDonald's is the best place in the world, but our oldest has begun to enjoy putting on a coat and a tie and going out to a nice restaurant with us as a grownup. Although we work hard to give each boy alone time, it is rare that a child will have a block of absolutely uninterrupted attention from both of us simultaneously. It seems this is a birthday gift they value, and so do we."

The remaining birthday traditions in this chapter fall in one of two categories. Either they are special ways to make a birthday festive or they are chronicling traditions that try to capture the passage of time.

Birthday Fairy

The magic moments of childhood are glitter on our growing years, remembered fondly when we are older. Some of us, like Lucy Lockhard, never outgrow a deep affection for magic and surprise, for wanting to sprinkle glitter on the everyday now and then. This tradition is for kindred spirits.

Along with the tooth fairy, the Easter bunny, and Santa Claus, the Lockhards have the birthday fairy, except everyone, even the littlest, knows who the birthday fairy is. "I just tell them," says Lucy, "that I always wanted to be a fairy and make magic, and birthdays are my chance.

"While you are sleeping, waiting to wake up to a happy, happy birthday, all my very good wishes for you give me magical energy to transform your room and deliver birthday presents."

The transformation is simple. A large sign, a dozen or more balloons, and some splashy gift wrapping on the birthday presents are the basics. "Anything else depends on how powerful the magic is at the moment. This correlates directly with what else is going on in our lives and how significant a birthday it is."

The Lockhard philosophy is that you should not have to wait all day to be surprised or worry that you've been forgotten. If the day begins deliciously, you can savor it all day long.

"After presents, we have birthday breakfast, which is usually something like fresh strawberries, fruit juice, and wonderful coffee cake." Lucy confesses to an ulterior motive in serving coffee cake. "I hate to cook and I'm not big on fancy dinners. I'd rather be a balloon-blowing fairy. This way, by 9 a.m., the work part of the party is over, the day has started out gloriously, and I don't have to spend all day fussing over dinner.

"I need to warn you," cautions Lucy, "based on my experiences growing up, that somewhere in adolescence your kids will think this is a wacko, dumb idea, because we had the birthday fairy in my house growing up. Don't stop. I came out the other end and was so hooked I made my college roommate be the birthday fairy."

Clue Birthdays

Here is a way of adding family involvement to gift giving.

If Roger Godding ever gives you a birthday present, you will not just unwrap it. None of the Goddings simply gives presents; they give each other exercises in mental agility. Before you can open your birthday present, you have to guess accurately what it is. You cannot open it until you guess. Sometimes you even have to find it, like the time $50 was frozen in the ice-cube tray.

Usually there is a poem to provide the clue or clues. Sometimes there are picture clues or object clues. It is *never* "Happy Birthday" from a greeting-card company.

"My father," says Roger, "was the master clue constructor. Since only the gift giver knows the gift, the whole family gets involved. It could take all day to figure out Dad's gifts. If you guessed in the middle of school, it was awful having to wait till after school to get Dad on the phone or, worse, to wait until he came home at night. The gift was really unimportant; it was the quest that was so much fun.

"One of my sister's very favorite gifts was a pair of shoelaces, not a spectacular gift for a fifteen-year-old, but this was her clue:

> *"The eyes can see*
> *How tied are we*
> *Knotted in affection.*
>
> *The tongues can say*
> *A Happy Birthday*
> *Wagging with affection.*
>
> *Let our souls insist*
> *This love exists*
> *With ties of affection."*

Birthday Squares

In Birthday Squares, each year is marked by making special squares for a memory quilt.

Tess and Joe Williamson live on a farm Tess's father owned. Both of them grew up in the heartland of America and lived seemingly stereotypical lives. Joe played high-school football, and Tess was a cheerleader. They were high-school sweethearts. Tess followed Joe to the state university. They married the June after she graduated and came home to prove you could still be a farmer in modern America. Just in case, Tess took her degree in education and landed a job teaching second grade in the local elementary school.

"Our traditions," says Tess, "are not very new. We are fortunate that we live close to our families, and our kids are growing up not too differently from the way Joe and I grew up. One big difference is my working. I love teaching, and the security of the salary relieves a lot of the tensions that come with farming. Both my mom and Joe's were full-time farm women. They always had big gardens and canned and quilted and baked, and it's natural for me to do those things, too; but during the school year I don't have a lot of time. I still can a tremendous amount in the summer, and the kids and I do lots of baking together all year round. Although I know a lot about quilting and love doing it, it was one thing that had fallen by the wayside, which is one reason the birthday squares give me so much pleasure."

The birthday squares started when Tess's first child was three. Patty is now eleven and has twenty-two squares. Her two younger sisters have fewer but, unlike Patty, have yet to contribute on their own.

When Patty was three, Tess made an embroidered square with the idea that eventually she would make a memory quilt. Now for every birthday there is a square from Tess and from the grandmothers as well. Special occasions may also prompt the making of a special square. Patty won a blue ribbon last year in a horse show and was so excited that she decided to make her own square to commemorate the event.

Tess says her squares are always secret. The girls can't see them until the day of their birthday, and it is a very special moment when a new square is unwrapped. Each square says something about an event during the year.

"This probably sounds corny," Tess says, "but I guess I always assumed I'd put the squares together when they got married. Now that I am saying it, I suppose I shouldn't assume they all will marry, but in the meantime this is our way of marking the years."

I was telling a friend about this tradition a little sorrowfully. It is such a nice idea, but one I am unequipped to carry out since I hate to sew and do it poorly. I could no more embroider anything worth preserving than grow six inches. My friend is not much of a seamstress either, but she is artistic and at least she has figured out how to thread her sewing machine properly. She got very excited about adapting Tess Williamson's idea by working with her kids to make squares.

They have begun to mark important family events by using fabric crayons to make very large squares, which my friend then backs and binds on her sewing machine. These will ultimately end up as a wall hanging.

It was fun to see someone picking up on one of these new traditions and adapting it to her own family. But I still did not see any fit for me with memory squares—until our trip to Bainbridge Island, two thousand miles from the Williamsons' farm.

The Lindahls are a different kind of farm family with a different way of making memory squares. The parents grew up in suburban Seattle, knowing nothing of farm life. Fourteen years ago they moved to an old house with a couple of acres on the island, wanting to simplify their life and live closer to the rhythms of nature. They plant fruit trees to commemorate important rites of passage and celebrate the winter solstice and the end of summer. They also do month squares. They showed me the month of June, each day indicated in a two-inch square on a piece of posterboard. In each square, a member of the family had drawn a picture and noted an event. June 11 read "Poochie has eight pups." June 17 had a picture of a mitt with the caption "John catches a fly ball," and June 19 simply said "Gorgeous sunset."

I knew we would not do a square every night, but it gave me a great idea for how to get my own memory squares. We wrote down all the super things that happened during our Seattle summer: Mom was forty; we went to a pig roast; Seth's first overnight camp; Mike learned gene splicing; trip to Victoria; Cousin Eliot came to visit. We made a board of squares, fitting each square with one of the labels from our list and a Magic Marker drawing. Then we did another board with important moments from our two-week trip home through national parks. I had these framed for our Seattle-summer souvenirs. A quilt would have been better, but this was possible.

The next two traditions are other unique ways of capturing important family events.

Family Portraits

When our first son was born, we bought a 16mm movie projector. When our second son was born, we upgraded our Instamatic. If we had had a third child, undoubtedly there would be no pictorial record of the occasion.

We are hopelesss. Nobody remembers the camera, and if someone does, there's no film. Life's greatest moments are recorded in our mind's eye but not in the photo album. That is why the Sullivan family's tradition is so appealing to me. This family celebrates major rites of passage with special family portraits.

The Sullivans are a large, noisy, funny family. There is lots of red hair and freckles, and the kids look as if they are waiting to be discovered by the people who design corn-flakes boxes.

Given their photogenic quality, it seems fitting that they honor rites of passage with a family portrait. Births, graduations, and any anniversary or birthday evenly divisible by five, which with four children is frequent, is occasion for a family portrait. There is a hired photographer of more or less professional status. Only once was it the sort who does things inside a studio. Usually, it is the friend of somebody's friend who is asked to take lots and lots of pictures. Then there is a major family conference over the proofs and, ultimately, one is chosen, blown up to 12″ x 14″, framed, and hung on the family-picture wall.

Everyone's family pictures are special, but the Sullivans' pictures are extra special because they do more than show what people look like. They are pictorial diaries, cluttered with favorite objects of the times. Five-year-olds clutch raggedy stuffed animals and ten-year-olds are decked out in hockey jackets lofting trophies. One year the family perched on Father's first major effort at home carpentry, a bookcase, and one year the kids insisted on sporting a banner that read: "Mom: Weight Watchers' Wonder."

Deciding what to wear and what to hold for these family portraits is serious business, requiring great family debate. "It is a nice way of reviewing what was really important to us during the year and what we value for ourselves and for us as a family," says Peg Sullivan quietly. She smiles at the portraits marching along the wall, exuding the life and energy that is the Sullivan family.

The Birthday Letter

The Birthday Letter is an annual summing-up letter from parents to child.

Howard Davidoff is a big, bearded teddy bear. He looks, accurately, like a holdout from the sixties poured into a faded turtleneck. His wife, Maggie Maxwell, is a connoisseur of antique clothing, who manages to look funky but fantastic in something of shiny velvet she bought for $12.50. Howard is an electronics whiz who mixes sound for television and tapes. Maggie volunteers with handicapped children and has a patience that works small miracles. They and their two young children live in an old house filled with an intriguing jumble that Maggie calls Period Eclectic.

Their birthday tradition, as much a gift for themselves as for the children, is one of my favorites.

Maggie has a book for each child, one of those pretty, cloth-bound books with empty pages inside. On each child's birthday, Howard and Maggie write the child a letter in his or her book about important family events of the year, what strikes each parent about the child, what their predictions and musings are, and whatever else seems fitting to write, including how loved the child is. A small picture goes with each letter.

The older child is only eight, so there are years and pages to go, but I, who don't know the child, loved reading the letters. I can imagine how delighted a child and the child's children will be someday to explore this birthday chronicle.

ANNIVERSARIES

Anniversaries must be the least celebrated rite of passage in the nation. Most people, however cheerfully married, appear to let this occasion slide past. When I first began interviewing to collect traditions I would ask, "What do you do for your anniversary?" Invariably, a long pause would follow.

Sometimes the response was "We go out to dinner." One lady said, "We do something together"—and then, sheepishly, "Like put in a new sewer pipe in the basement," thus aptly characterizing what lots of couples consider a reasonable anniversary celebration.

It was clear that my question was making people feel embarrassed or apologetic. I began by saying, "It seems most couples do very little to mark their anniversaries. How about you?"

There must be people out there who at least buy presents, husbands who enjoy giving their wives gorgeous pieces of jewelry or books of poetry, playful wives who slip into their local department store and come home with titillating nightgowns or who buy bikini underwear for their husbands. (Do write if you do stuff like that, because you are devilishly hard to find!)

Anniversary traditions are scarce. There are, of course, lots of couples who always go to dinner with particular friends or always go to a special restaurant by themselves. Going out to dinner for an anniversary or birthday or graduation is nearly custom in some quarters, it is so prevalent. I love being taken out to a fine restaurant, or even a good greasy spoon, and I commend that as an excellent way to celebrate anything—like Wednesdays—but it hardly qualifies as a new tradition.

Even nicer is having someone swoop you away for a week or a weekend. Some couples use their anniversary as a welcome excuse for time away together. It requires more time and money than imagination to carry off an annual anniversary escape, but it need not be an expensive holiday far away. It might just be overnight somewhere close. Making it a tradition to take yourselves away for "us time" every year, whether around an anniversary, a birthday, or a holiday, is a lovely way to say "We're special." Our family life gets so crowded that Michael and I can forget to make time to catch up with each other. Paying attention to these calendar-connected events is a built-in way of scheduling personal time for romance.

Although I am touting elegant dinners and private escapes as a prelude to more unusual ideas, do not despair if your anniversaries have never seen solicitous waiters or hotel desk clerks. Stop instantly if you have harbored guilt, disappointment, or feelings of inadequacy because anniversaries were non-events. Non-observance may be a national tradition.

The Anniversary Fund

In this tradition, each anniversary is a means toward a shared love of travel.

Chuck and Carole Peterson decided early in their marriage that making money was not their major focus. Chuck is a New England prep-school teacher who is infinitely patient helping squirmy thirteen-year-olds discover the excitement of literature. He is also an outdoorsman who cherishes the time teaching allows for hiking and fishing, raising a superb garden, and paying attention to the passing seasons. Carole is a professional potter and amateur weaver who has warmed their house—and their life—with her work.

They find their life satisfying, and their children have been enriched by growing up with literature and nature and art as much a part of every week as breakfast. Mostly the Petersons do not mind being what Chuck calls "a little to the left of affluent." Only their desire to travel made Chuck and Carole fret over money.

"I don't mind not eating out much, and I certainly don't mind living in jeans," says Carole. "I don't even mind watching pennies at the supermarket if I know all of life is not going to be penny-pinching. Our anniversary fund helps me through the really pinchy times."

The anniversary fund is a tradition that evolved very early in the Petersons' marriage. "When we first got married," says Chuck, "we were too young and romantic to let an anniversary just slide by but too poor to manage much more than pizza and a movie."

"So," says Carole, "we decided on layaway romance. All year, each of us squirrels away small sums of money. If I am offered a class to teach and I don't want to but think I should take it for the money, I stash a portion of the money. If Chuck does some unexpected tutoring and we don't have a household crisis, he will hold back a little. Sometimes, when I'm about to buy something, I'll decide I don't need it and put the money away. We do not let this rule our lives, mind you. Most of the time we hardly talk about it, but each of us has developed the habit of tucking a $1, $5, or $10 bill away whenever . . . We never count it until our anniversary. Then we make a great ceremony of adding it up to be deposited in our special account.

"It is absolutely sacrosanct not to use that account for anything. It is not a family savings account. The anniversary fund is ours, and we have only borrowed from it once in seventeen years. We don't put in much. I think the most we ever deposited in one year was about $670. The least must have been about $156. That was a bad year.

"Our deal is that, every fifth anniversary, we take the whole account and spend it on a trip for just the two of us. I suppose if we only had $50, we would spend it on a night in a hotel, but we would do something."

Chuck and Carole have been married seventeen years and have traveled in between the anniversary trips, but both say the anniversary trips have been special. In 1970, they spent ten days in England. In 1975, Chuck says they needed unrelieved relaxation and chose California. "We drank iced tea on the beach, had room service for breakfast, and luxuriated till we ran out of money. In 1980, we went to Alaska, which was exciting. If we can manage," says Chuck, "we want to go to Japan in 1985."

Now that the kids are older, they have started contributing to the fund as anniversary or birthday gifts for their parents. "That has been lovely," says Carole, "and now our oldest son has started his own trip account. He yearns to go be a Viking in Norway one summer. Why not?"

I like the Petersons' way of celebrating because it is so reflective of a good marriage—building together through good times and bad. But once every five years may be too deferred a gratification for some people.

In this next example, one woman has decided how to deal with the fact that her husband is unlikely to plan the anniversaries she fantasizes.

Plan a Fantasy

Sheila is the mother with Once-a-Week Days who came to the dramatic awareness that it was not her sole responsibility to see that each member of the family was happy.

She is a person who needs order and structure in her life

to keep her from worrying about how things will work out, but she also needs fantasy. In the way of the superorganized, she has structured it into a system that builds on her theme of individual responsibility.

Sheila and her husband take turns planning their anniversary, but instead of trying first to please the other, each plans what he or she thinks is an ideal celebration.

"This way I get to buy myself things I like that Pete would never think to buy me. Last year, for example, I planned a Japanese evening. I ordered dinner from a Japanese restaurant and brought the food home. I bought myself a beautiful kimono, and I arranged for the children to spend the night at their cousins'. After dinner, I gave Pete an oil back rub before a Japanese-style bath."

By contrast, the year before, Pete rented indoor tennis court space, invited friends, and threw a beer, barbecue, and tennis party, which Sheila enjoyed but not as much as her kimono. "I guess our anniversary gift to each other really is indulging each other's whims or fantasies. Pete would never plan a kimono and oil rub, but I don't have to go through life wishing he would."

Every-Month Anniversaries

For those of us who don't celebrate anniversaries at all, this tradition may be overwhelming. I'm not sure it is a tradition that can sustain itself for decades, but the pleasure of a good marriage after a bad one has been a powerful impetus for these people.

Callie O'Conner was married at nineteen, became a mother at twenty-one, and tried to play dutiful domestic wife to a husband who was seldom home. It took a decade for her frustration to build up enough steam to blast her into a different life-style. She divorced, moved her children to an apartment in the city, and got a job. Today she makes a living as a magazine photographer and is married to Tom, a local television producer. They live in the middle of the city in a seventeen-room mansion of fading elegance which they bought very cheaply.

They have filled the house with Callie's daughters, thirteen and seventeen, a surrogate daughter, a resident rock band, an assortment of stray passersby, and several animals. Another friend occupies the carriage house. "We are not allowed to rent out rooms, but there is no ban on having servants," says Tom. So when the rock band is home, the members earn their keep by plastering, painting, and generally keeping the house from rack and ruin. "Besides," adds Tom, "people are cheaper and more fun than a burglar-alarm system."

Callie and Tom have been married four years. Tom, who is several years younger than Callie, is quiet and articulate. He talked about the difficulty of moving into the sphere of three strong women, one well launched into adolescence, and about meshing with their lives. He talked about his own painful custody fight and the warmth of the household for his son when he visits.

It is a busy household, with people going in diverse directions at different times. Tom may start work at 5 a.m. and Callie may not finish until 7 or 8 p.m. The girls have the usual complicated teenage schedules. "What keeps us together as a strong family is a philosophy and a commitment, an attitude to be a family. We are not really organized enough for traditions," mused Callie, who went on to talk about pancakes on Shrove Tuesday and green St. Patrick's Day dinners and extravagant birthdays and elaborate Thanksgivings and Easter egg hunts and Chinese New Year's parties.

"What about anniversaries?" I asked. Tom and Callie exchanged glances. "Yes," said Callie, "we celebrate our anniversary. Every month."

"Every month," said I.

"Ummm, every month, every eleventh," said Tom. "We always do something for each other. It might be a present under the pillow, a note at work, a special dinner, but always something. One month we took a picnic of strawberries and champagne to the park at midnight."

"One of the best," reminisced Callie, "was the pitcher of cold margaritas Tom brought to the hospital the night before some minor surgery."

I wondered aloud how such busy people found time to remember month after month. "Once you're into doing it," explained Callie, "you just plan for it. I collect little gifts when I see them and tuck them away for the eleventh or store up ideas driving to work. It does not take so much time to make a few minutes special."

Tom and Callie have known other, less happy times, and celebrating each eleventh is a way of underscoring how important their marriage is for them.

Come-Away-with-Me Anniversary

I went into my "Nobody celebrates anniversaries so don't feel bad if you don't, but do you?" routine. And Trudy Kinderly said, "Well, we celebrate! Anniversaries are absolutely big doings in our house."

Howie Kinderly is a successful accountant with Sol Hurok tendencies, and Howie likes to do things in style. "We always go away, just the two of us, as an anniversary present, and Howie does the planning in his own way. I have found out about these trips in all sorts of bizarre ways. Once I came home and tripped over my luggage in the front hall. I've gotten plants inviting me to flourish in the sun with Howie, and candy boxes and singing telegrams. The most amazing one was the morning I arrived at work and found a manila envelope on my desk labled "Open Immediately—Urgent." I thought, Oh, Lord, what do I need to do now, opened it, and found an intimate letter from Howie inviting me to Hawaii, plus an itinerary. My boss knew; everything was arranged. It's very exciting."

As I wrote about the Kinderlys, I found myself wondering if I should paste this page on the bathroom mirror as a subtle message to my husband. Michael is a wonderful, caring husband, but the odds of his masterminding a surprise trip to Hawaii are stiffer than a carnival game wheel. The strategy for women in my shoes, I decided, is to be Howies themselves. Who says it is always the man's role to mastermind an anniversary vacation? And outside of Seattle, I found a woman who really had made that philosophy work. She takes her husband out for a date on their anniversary. She sends him a single yellow rose at the office, tells him what time to be ready (and expects him to hire the sitter, whom she takes home), drives, and pays the bill. "I plan the evening and take him out. We have a wonderful time."

A Dating Game

A woman in New Jersey laughingly shared an unusual anniversary tradition. "On the date that we first met, we celebrate by going to the same restaurant we went to that first night. My husband picks me up at the house as if he were calling for me for the first time. We pretend the entire evening that we have just met, and we tell each other about ourselves as if we don't know each other."

BAR MITZVAH AND CONFIRMATION

Religious ceremony need not follow traditional forms if those forms will cause a family to reject the entire process. Rather, traditions can be adapted and personalized so that the participants find the comfort level necessary to allow them to participate.

Self-styled Bar Mitzvah

In ancient times, a bar mitzvah was no more than the Sabbath morning a young man took his turn reading from the Torah with the other adult males. After that, he could be counted in the *minyan*, as one of the ten men needed to begin services.

Today, a bar or bat mitzvah when the child is thirteen hardly signifies his or her attainment of adulthood, but in many families it is an important milestone, a ceremony that induces a child to study, connects him or her to the past, and brings relatives together. Like baptism, consecration, or confirmation, it affirms membership in the group.

Conventionally, a student prepares for bar or bat mitzvah by attending Hebrew classes two days a week after school for several years and, finally, by memorizing a portion of the Bible in Hebrew to read in temple on the day chosen, the bar mitzvah morning.

Ruth and Seth Kolodney found themselves with conflicting feelings about this traditional ritual. They liked the idea of extending through their children a continuous bond with the past. They wanted their children to have a clear sense of their religious heritage and to be knowledgeable and proud of that history, but they themselves were not an observant family. Although they observed religious holidays, such observance was informal. They had not joined any of the organized religious institutions in Chicago, and they were not firm enough in their own beliefs to wage a very successful fight with their son, Daniel, who did not cotton to the idea of spending two precious afternoons each week in Hebrew class.

Like some Catholic and Protestant as well as Jewish families, the Kolodneys were not comfortable with the traditional organized church or synagogue, but they wanted—needed—something for themselves and their children.

"I want our children to be proud and knowledgeable of our religion and tolerant and respectful of others'," Ruth Kolodney said. "I don't want them to feel cheated because we gave them nothing. Yet I don't feel it is right to have them taught rules we won't reinforce or to attend institutions we don't attend.

"Instead of enrolling Daniel in the usual after-school class, we told him we wanted him bar mitzvahed but it was up to him and a tutor to decide what form it would take and when Daniel was ready. Then we went searching for a tutor. We wanted a man, someone who could be a role model and special friend. We wanted someone very knowledgeable but capable of relating to a young boy, someone whose views, if not like ours, were at least not contradictory to ours and someone likely to be in Chicago at least three years. We were lucky. We found a young man who was an ordained Reform rabbi working on a Ph.D. in philosophy. For at least an hour every week for two and a half years, he met with Daniel. Daniel had a small assignment each week as well. After the time with Daniel, his tutor came downstairs and had coffee with us and gave us an education, too. Together we all learned. We all had a hand in planning the ceremony, although Daniel kept his talk on what Judaism meant to him a surprise.

"It was a very proud, moving day; but more important, the preparation was a growing process for all of us. Daniel was not told what to do. He had to work it out for himself and that demanded knowledge and thought and, ultimately, commitment."

Tangible Affirmation

Church confirmation, a related rite-of-passage occasion, prompted a different but equally creative response by the Bollings. In their Protestant church, confirmation is a reaffirmation of commitment, a time when young people first stand to make a commitment to the church for themselves. "Theoretically," Paul Bolling explained, "it should be a very significant event. In fact, it has taken on a certain perfunctory quality in our church. To us, our commitment to the church, to Christian values, and to God are significant and vital parts of our lives, and we wanted this act by our children, as they move toward adulthood, to be significant. We decided that with the confirmation of each child we would make a gift to our church in honor of that child. The gift is not money. It is a tangible thing and it is something the children feel is important. They spend a great deal of time weighing what gift they want to make. We ask that each child earn $20 toward the gift."

A gift, as Paul explained, can be small or large. It can be a single book for the library or a piece of art; it can be repainting a classroom, adding a needed lamp, or, as one of his children chose, giving art supplies for the little people's Sunday school. If one can afford it, it can be a computer, a special lecturer, flowers for the pulpit, but it can just as effectively be an embroidered bookmark or a new can opener for the kitchen.

"We like the tradition," Paul went on, "because it gives the children an enlarged sense of ownership in the church and a sense that it is our house to care for."

GRADUATION

Because graduation is the culmination of so much that is intensely personal, I am taken with a tradition that friends of ours invented, the personal diploma.

Personal Diploma

Max and Sheila Bloom designed their own personal diploma to complement their son Skip's institutional one. In contrast to the somber black lettering on white parchment, this diploma is elaborately decorated with a colorful and intricate border that looks at first like a fruit-and-flower design but, on closer inspection, is interspersed with footballs, football helmets, and baseball mitts.

The text, done in calligraphy, is long and personal. It celebrates Skip's six high-school years, including his adolescent compulsions, successes, and failures. Max and Sheila managed to touch on shaving, driving, dating, and working, as well as math, music, English literature, and football, football, football, and special family times.

The diploma begins:

To our son Thaddeus "Skip" Bloom on his graduation on this, the 5th day of June, 1982, we present this diploma in honor of six rich, and sometimes arduous, years at _____ High School.

As you collect this diploma and move on to the next stage of your development, we, your loving and proud parents, remember the vivid moments of these important years: . . .

The Blooms wrote the text themselves and found a local artist to design their diploma. It is beautifully framed and now hangs in Skip's room at college. This tradition pleases me because it was stimulated by this book, and it is just the kind of personal and creative response that produces the warmth and satisfaction and pleasure we all want in our families.

5

National Holidays

Some folks object to a lot of our national holidays. Nothing but a bunch of media hype for commercialism, they mutter; they'd have us stand up and say balderdash to Mother's Day cards, candy valentines, and $14.95 rubber Halloween masks. Yet others are delighted with one more excuse to celebrate.

By now, it is clear where I stand. I am pleased to have an externally imposed structure that impels me to give thanks, honor Dad, and salute Eros. I welcome the fact that the calendar clears and points us away from our separate activities and toward family. So long as I don't have to cook for every one of these events, I am happy to have them at regularly spaced intervals.

In fact, my problem is not that I object to these occasions but that I tend to take them seriously, that I want them to have a significance that requires more than buying a turkey, a tie, or a box of candy. I cannot do them all with equal zest, so I favor a few. Thanksgiving is my favorite, my special holiday. It is the one for which I always cook cheerfully. Halloween is my stand on creativity. Much to my children's dismay, I insist on homemade costumes, which they have to make. Since I do not sew, we have all gotten very good with cardboard cartons. New Year's is a special time for old friends. The rest are still awaiting inspiration.

What follows is a potpourri of people's ideas for the national holidays that inspire them. Like the calendar, we'll begin with New Year's Eve.

New Year's Eve is supposed to be an occasion and so we worry about how we are going to spend it. Should we have a party, or hope we get invited to one? Should we go out or stay home?

The New Year's Annual Review Resolution

As a teenager, I used to make long lists of New Year's resolutions: I won't bite my nails; I'll give up eating chocolate; I won't punch my brother; I'll study my French vocabulary more. Of course, I was dreadful about carrying these out and never had a flush of success. In later years, I decided it made more sense to have just one New Year's resolution and concentrate on that. For ten years now it has been "Lose weight." In fact, as I think about it, it has become a tradition—not one I recommend. Instead, I like what the Hollands do much better.

Nina Holland says it was too hard to find a baby-sitter when the kids were little, so she and Derick gave up on going out. "We would have a bottle of champagne together and sort of review the year. And then we found we always ended up planning the next year, talking about what we hoped would happen, where we wanted to go.

"Without our thinking about it, it became a tradition for New Year's Eve to be an annual review and planning session. Even when the kids were old enough not to need sitters, we found we wanted to be home. It's a wonderful evening. The phone never rings. It's cold outside and snuggly inside and the perfect time to talk about the future.

"Now the children join us, and we make resolutions for the

family, things we all want to happen. The resolutions are not behaviors, they are tangible events we know we can make happen if we work at it. For example, one year we realized we had small children and no wills. That was our resolution: make wills and make sure our affairs were in order. My own resolution that same year was to splice all the movie films together on big reels. I can't tell you the sense of accomplishment it gave me to get that done.

"One year our family resolution was to relandscape the front of the house. This actually came from the kids, who were more bothered by the overgrowth than we were.

"Last year on New Year's Eve, we ended up with a surprise resolution, one we had not really considered before that evening. We resolved to take a family trip to Europe before our eldest graduates high school in two years, and we are all working to make it happen. So big things can begin on New Year's Eve."

Nina Holland says she thinks a trick of this tradition is only to resolve to do the doable. "If you fail, it takes some of the fun out of planning, so we try to resolve to do things we know we can and really want to do."

For the Holllands, success has strengthened their tradition and strengthened their family as well.

Mother as Guest

Another holiday we know we are supposed to do something for is Mother's Day. Some mothers may be mature enough to recognize that commercialism inspires this event and that every day should be Mother's Day. I, however, will take whatever extra catering I can get, which is why I like the following.

The Sibbons have four sons, competent, articulate kids who sometimes regard their parents, Barry and Natalie, as androids.

Never mind that Barry is a successful psychologist and Natalie is a skilled speech therapist, they are still parents. The kids' periodic disdain notwithstanding, they are a nice family. The youngest, Richard, is a college freshman, the two middle ones are in graduate school, and the oldest, Paul, manages a restaurant. They seem very together as a family, so I was anxious to interview them. But it was only with great difficulty that I was able to tease out this special tradition that fits young families well.

When I explained what I was looking for, Natalie started to laugh. "Where were you when we needed you? We are just old enough that we did not talk about these things as a family when we needed to. I guess I tried to institute traditions. And everybody else kind of fell in line," she said apologetically. A little while later, she said, "Gee, I am realizing what a boring, uncreative family we have been . . . We didn't have much money when the kids were young and most of our traditions sprang from that: everybody had chores, everybody did yard work, and everybody learned to bake because store-bought goods were forbidden. Every year we took a camping trip right after school finished in June. We really have no interesting traditions."

In spite of her protestations, a picture of a family life filled with bonding emerged. Everyone sat down to breakfast and dinner together, everyone tackled projects together, everyone went out together. Natalie orchestrated all these events. But one tradition grew up that she did not orchestrate and that, in a quiet way, let her know her efforts were appreciated.

On Natalie's birthday and on Mother's Day, Barry and the kids make dinner. It began when Richard was three. At first, says Natalie, it was stuff like pizza and hot dogs. As the kids got older, the meals got better. "In honesty, as the kids took over from Barry, the quality improved. Barry is great on minds, but death on food.

"At first, it was hard not to meddle. I would want to go into the kitchen and supervise so they would do it right. Barry would kick me out. Over the years, I finally learned how to be a gracious receiver. It's hard, you know, when you are used to being a giver. I learned not to put a foot in the kitchen either for cooking or for cleanup, and no matter what came out, I didn't criticize. I even learned to refrain from constructive suggestion. The kids put out some fabulous meals, and I loved it. This birthday, for the first time, all the kids were gone and Barry took me to an elegant restaurant for my fifty-second birthday. It wasn't as good."

As we finished talking, Natalie observed that they were ready for "a second stage of traditions. I think we can do better if we think it out consciously and collectively this time."

SOS Homemade Cards

Mother's Day, Father's Day, anniversaries, and birthdays support the greeting-card industry. They would also like us to remember Halloween, Thanksgiving, St. Patrick's Day, etc. This next tradition believes in cards but not profits for the card manufacturers.

Many of us have office walls hung with pictures our children did while we tried to squeeze in a few extra hours of work. This tradition had just such diversionary beginnings.

Hal Smith is a graphic designer. A lilting Jamaican accent, Belafonte-like build, and smiling eyes give him a romantic, carefree air, belying his intensity about his work and his fifteen-year-old son, for whom he has been a single parent for ten years.

When Alex was little, Hal would frequently bring him to the office Saturday morning and give him paper and pencil to occupy himself. To keep Alex involved and busy, whenever there was a birthday or holiday, Hal would get his son started making cards for grandparents, aunts, and uncles. And, of course, Hal's paper scraps and colored pencils were much more interesting than those of your average doctor, lawyer, or executive. Out of them came the SOS tradition, so named when Alex decided his cards needed an imprint competitive with those of commercial card makers.

SOS stands for Smith's Original Sentiments, homemade greetings produced annually for grandparents and parents on Mother's Day, Father's Day, birthdays, and Valentine's Day. SOS produces randomly for other occasions, but its core is the grandchild-to-grandparent relationship. In his ten productive years, Alex has progressed from nursery-school abstractionist to this year's three-dimensional Valentine's Day sculpture with moving parts. Alex and Hal worked cooperatively on this for weeks.

"The cards have served us well in many ways," says Hal. "First, the grandparents adore them. Rather than my buying a gift for Alex to give when he was little, these were really his gifts. They showed him growing up and reflected his personality. And the cards are just the kind of thing a proud grandmother can show off with delight.

"Second, it gave Alex some responsibility. He did not have to depend on me or his baby-sitter to organize him. He could do it himself and get the pleasure of giving his own.

"Third, in recent years, it has become a project Alex and I can do together. The ideas are still his, but as his visions have become more elaborate, he's organized me as an assistant. I try not to play teacher, although occasionally I slip in a little design lesson. Mainly, it is fun for us to work together. Doing the Valentine sculpture was terrific, and in between working, there was a relaxed time for me and Alex to talk, which is getting harder as he grows older."

A year ago, Hal selected some of Alex's cards that various family members had saved, arranged them spectacularly between two tall sheets of clear plastic, and hung them in an entryway as a personal SOS for ongoing family ties and traditions.

Flowers, Candy, and Valentine's Escape

Valentine's Day is another holiday with a big commercial hype. Mushy as the sentiment is, I like it. It is a little silly, but it is fun. Bob Cohn likes it, too.

When Bob Cohn was a nineteen-year-old sophomore at Northwestern, he wanted to go into the family business, get married, and have five children. He was unusually family-oriented for a handsome teenager, and it has only gotten worse over the years. He delights in choosing gifts, sending flowers, and relaxing in the warmth of his family.

He adores his wife and his two daughters. (His wife says the dog and two cats will have to do in lieu of the extra children.) And although he does not want the girls to grow up soft or spoiled, he's a doting daddy.

The Cohns' favorite tradition centers on Valentine's Day. Bob sends flowers to his daughters and buys them nightgowns, the kind his wife, Lee, says only a grandmother or a smitten father would ever spend money for. And he brings home heart-shaped boxes of candy. I once asked him, says Lee, what he would do if we had a son. "Well, I hope not nightgowns, but I'd treat him specially. This is a time of year," says Bob, "when I really do spoil the girls and for once Lee lets me. I want them to look for a companion when they grow up that is able to give a lot of himself personally. I guess I feel if I set the scene, it will set a standard for them. I think they will be smart enough to understand that the caring and the effort are more important than the gifts."

The girls don't compete with Mommy on Valentine's Day because Daddy has a nice way of making it clear that Mom is still his number-one girl. On the Friday closest to Valentine's Day, Lee and Bob check into a hotel about two miles away. The hotel, decorated in the manner of an English country home, is as romantic an escape as you can find in the city and half the price on weekends that it is on weekdays. "We check in around 4 p.m. on Friday or whenever Bob can get away," says Lee. "Maybe we meet friends for dinner or go to a movie. One year in a snowstorm we just ordered tons of food from room service and had a wonderful time. We have breakfast the next morning and are home by noon.

"It's not even twenty-four hours away, but we've been doing it for seven years now, and we both look forward to it. It lets the kids know we value being alone with each other and somehow being in a different setting promotes different kinds of conversation, even different sex."

"One year Lee had a terrible cold. She brought her vaporizer," says Bob, "and went to bed at seven. I went out to a movie alone. But even that was worth it. I guess it shows a guy loves you a lot to buy a hotel room for your vaporizer."

My very favorite national holiday is Thanksgiving. Michael and I were married Thanksgiving eve, and Thanksgiving dinner has always been our time to celebrate. The following are appealing additions to the day.

Stuffing the Photo Album

After the big Thanksgiving dinner at the Striken house, everyone just sits—too stuffed to move, too sleepy to clean up, too embarrassed to go to bed at 7 p.m. This, says Nan Striken, is the perfect moment to send her daughter Jennifer upstairs to get the picture box.

"The picture box is where we drop family photos all year. You know, the ones we're planning to organize in an album but never do. They pile up for months, all jumbled together. Then, on Thanksgiving, we get out the box and have a wonderful time sorting through, passing pictures around, and reminiscing about the year. The children are always delighted to relive their own special moments, and I am always surprised at how quickly I forget some of the good times we've had. I make sure to have a couple of empty albums on hand, and as we're talking we pop the best pictures right in.

"By the time we've finished, everyone is feeling good. Now the album stuffing is as much a part of our Thanksgiving celebration as the turkey stuffing."

The Neighborhood Football Game

I have never met Bill Baxter, but I know his neighbors, who describe him as a football fan and a family man, in that order. In the service of both, the Baxters began a neighborhood Thanksgiving tradition that gets the whole block in shape for Thanksgiving dinner. Every house on both sides of the street receives a flyer, delivered by the Baxter children, announcing this momentous athletic competition: the Thanksgiving family football game.

A little before ten, people start straggling up to the school playground, coffee cups in hand, with thermoses of hot apple cider, hot chocolate, and more coffee.

In some mysterious fashion, by 10:30, the assembled are divided into two teams and the players assault the field. Everyone plays, all ages, all sexes, and each team has its quota of toddlers to confuse the opposition. A Harpo Marx version of family football ensues, with lots of cheering and ample substitutions.

The game has been postponed because of rain but not snow.

One year it was played in three inches of snow with a deflated ball.

The Baxters provide enough doughnuts to feed a platoon, and for an hour or so there is laughter and fellowship and enough exercise to justify eating two kinds of pie for Thanksgiving dinner.

✳

There are several Fourth of July versions to this tradition, substituting baseball for football. In Seattle, boating and hiking are popular alternatives. One group has an annual Fourth of July canoe trip to an island for an enormous picnic. Each year, the group grows larger as friends' friends join and invite their friends, but it doesn't seem to matter.

Neighborhood get-togethers need not be confined to national holidays. We were invited to dinner one Sunday and found ourselves at a neighborhood community center, a small open area with a community pool, some playing fields, and picnic tables and rest rooms. Every summer Sunday around four there is a neighborhood softball game, followed by a potluck. Each family brings its own hot dogs to grill and a covered dish to share. The teenagers start the grill and the younger kids usually do the grilling, with discreet supervision. It is an easy, enjoyable evening for the adults and a favorite activity for the children.

Back to Thanksgiving and one more tradition that shifts away from food for a moment and focuses on the ideas behind the holiday.

Thanksgiving Reading

I had heard about the Ragnoles' Thanksgiving from a family that had been the invited guests one year. I called Ann Ragnole to ask if she would tell me about it. She was surprised. "I'd never thought of it as a new tradition before, but if your criteria are something our children will remember, something that is important to us as a family, and something we invented to fill a family need, this certainly qualifies. We both have families in St. Louis and I am the lynchpin. Thanksgiving is a way to pull the families together, but it's a risky business. There is always the danger of having people go at each other in awful discussions. Our families could not be more different. Paul is Italian Catholic. His parents are immigrants who are still very traditional. My family is as WASP as you can get. I'm a third-generation American, and my mother gets mail from the DAR.

"My solution is to dilute this pretty potent brew. I always invite another family with children, often someone new to the city, and some of my students from the university. I try, too, to have someone from another country.

"Having assembled this crowd for a holiday dinner, it seemed years ago—and still does—that we ought to make something of it. What has evolved is a pretty standard format, although the content changes year to year. The children share in reading a psalm and then in a reading that has something to do with Thanksgiving. Paul and I used to select the material, but now the kids are old enough [twelve, thirteen, and fifteen] to select and arrange it themselves. I'm their resource consultant. Paul says a semi-grace that talks about giving thanks for our good fortune, and I read a poem about welcoming friends. Over dinner we share what we are most thankful for during the year and make wishes for the world for the coming year. Depending on our guests, we may end up singing."

How many of us, far from family, have friends who serve as surrogate relatives? We share good times with them, sometimes only seeing them on these special occasions, but know we can count on them in a crunch.

I heard stories of special, stable friendships: two families that always have a coffee klatch on December 24, once at an airport, once at a hospital; four families that rotate hosting annual holidays; seven displaced Tennesseans whose families flee New York City for one's country farmhouse every Thanksgiving; a group of Chinese families that "do" Chinese New Years. These and others gave testimony to the importance of sharing together, of enlarging our numbers to amplify the festive notes. Fourth of July, Labor Day, Memorial Day, Thanksgiving, these are all good times for potluck suppers and outdoor picnics.

A Family of Friends

I encountered this tradition first in bits and pieces. Several people I interviewed in St. Louis mentioned something about a Sunday-evening potluck group that seemed to arouse a little envy among those who knew of it but were not included.

When I tracked down its originators, Sue and Joe Redingfeld, I discovered a macro-tradition, a tradition of traditions. I, too, felt a tug of envy over the large and diverse support system that has come to function as an extended family. In the four years the group has been together, its members have found compatibility and warmth, and they have been willing to invest energy in working through differences among people related only by choice.

The Redingfelds, who have two teenagers, are not displaced from family. Both sets of parents live only a few miles away. This nuclear group is the core for five other families, all of whom live in the Redingfelds' neighborhood, and two single friends. These are the regulars who come together every Sunday night for pot-luck dinner. It is usually held at the Redingfelds'. They have a large country kitchen, a roaring fireplace in the winter, a shady deck in the summer, and an extrovert's pleasure in people and tumult. "Sometimes," says Sue, "someone else will ask to have us, or I will ask that it be elsewhere, but usually it is here; people just know where to come.

"The kids have to have done their homework. Everyone brings something, but we never know what. Whatever shows up is what we eat for dinner. We use paper plates, everyone pitches in to clean up, especially kids and husbands, and it's over by 9 p.m.

"All our birthdays, kids' and adults', are celebrated at Sunday potluck and everyone's anniversaries. We have cake and candles and usually it is *the* party for the celebrant. Our parents serve as grandparents to all the families, none of whom have local grandparents. Because we all have different interests, we trade off children sometimes so kids get to do things their parents might not enjoy.

"On Memorial Day we all go to our place in the country, pitch tents, canoe down the river, and have a hayride hitched to the tractor. Every summer, we pile into three vans and make a Sunday afternoon of heading for a favorite fish-fry place in the next state. The Sunday before Christmas we always go caroling in the neighborhood between an early dinner and a late dessert. Those who don't go to visit family or have family in for Thanksgiving share it together. Last summer we rented a huge house at the ocean and spent a week together. This year we all wanted to go different places, so we are, and we're checking on good possibilities for the group in the future. Christmas Eve we spend alone with our families, but we always spend New Year's together. Everybody makes everybody something, perhaps a Christmas ornament. Husbands may do something on the lathe or give work time on the country place we all enjoy. David plays in the orchestra, so he gave us a concert last year. Howard is a photographer and every year he gives us a group photo he's taken sometime during the year. One of us will run a workshop on something—like framing—for the kids so they can make gifts."

Who are these people who want so much togetherness? They are hardworking souls "who do a lot of heavy mental work during the week, lead complicated lives, and need a support system." They are school heads and filmmakers, musicians and newspaper editors, and artists and teachers, all people who pour great energy into their work but are not especially well paid. "We were all into the formal entertainment, nice-dinner-party groove, but we couldn't afford it," says Sue. "The house had to be clean, or you had to pay a baby-sitter, and it didn't make sense. Even going to the movies was expensive. We all live in the same neighborhood and this seemed a much more sensible way to have fun. Nobody feels he has to come if he doesn't want to. It's perfectly acceptable to stay home or do something else or bring a guest. We all come because we feel a need to be there."

About a year ago, the six women who have families began meeting for breakfast on Monday morning. "We meet at 7:30 and are at work by nine. This is our time to talk about women things. Every time we get into a discussion about sex, the GE repairmen at the next table can't move. It started because we never felt we had enough time to talk women's issues on Sunday nights. Now we just separate that out and deal with it in its own time."

In the three years, one family has left the group because of personal problems, and one family, which had moved from the neighborhood and returned, joined.

Many of us will envy being able to find such a group of warm and caring friends, but few of us would invest the energy and the time that Sue and Joe Redingfeld gave to getting the group started.

There are many variations on this theme and I was inspired to invent one, but inspiration alone is not enough. I, as the family extrovert, like a steady diet of people. There is not enough time to see all the people I enjoy, but I have less and less patience for arranging dinner parties. My husband, who is an introvert, finds there is never enough quiet time for reading and thinking. The very thought of thirty-three people every Sunday night left him gray. We decided, or rather I decided and he acquiesced, to use three holidays a year as an agreed time to invite friends and their children to an informal potluck supper and to let them know they were welcome to bring guests. We chose Labor Day, Valentine's Day, and Memorial Day as good times for informal coming together, for keeping in touch with people we like but seldom see, for including foreign visitors, graduate students, and neighbors. Labor Day and Valentine's Day have now passed unceremoniously. I am not betting on Memorial Day. Sometimes the reason other people have these good ideas and not us is that they really aren't such good ideas for us.

6

Single-Parent Traditions

I T IS TOUGH to be a single parent. To whom can you say, "You deal with it . . ." or "On your way home from work, would you . . ."? Nearly six million parents are bringing up children without a supporting spouse. But if it is not uncommon anymore to have only one parent at home, it is still hard. There is a sense of loss. There must also be joy and laughter and the awareness that people are a family whatever their arrangement. It is caring and commitment and sharing and loving that make a family, not numbers.

When divorce or death disrupts established patterns, it is important to avoid a vacuum. New family arrangements call for new traditions.

The following traditions focus on special problems, special difficult times that single parents encounter, but they have applications for married people, too.

Guess Who's Coming to Dinner

Cary Chen's daughters are both in college now, intelligent young women Cary can talk with as friends. "We were talking last summer and my eldest said, 'You know, Mom, the trouble with us is that we didn't think we were a good family. We thought we were defective, but it wasn't true.' She is right, and it was my fault. I got divorced long before it was fashionable. I felt my dreams hadn't materialized, that I was cheating the girls. It's only now that I'm coming to see the folly of that logic, but I spent a long time savoring self-pity.

"There was one thing I really did right. After the divorce, life seemed too narrow. There was my work and the house and the girls. I hardly dated and few new people intersected our lives. So for all the years the girls were in school, a couple of times each month, I would invite social people to dinner—role models, heroes or heroines, or just interesting characters. I explained to people why I was inviting them—I had to be honest because I didn't know most of these people very well. I was careful not to use them to fill my own social needs, and I think people gratefully sensed that. Generally, people were flattered to be invited. I'd ask them to come to talk about their work or whatever they did that made them special. And I insisted that the girls sit at the table, ask questions, and act interested, whether they were or not. They met dozens of different people and sometimes their families this way.

"I believe it impacted on them substantially. They are poised, articulate, interesting young adults, far more so than I was at their age, and they have more adult contacts in the community than they would otherwise. Although I did not have the good sense to see it at the time, we really can say now, 'We are a special family.' "

Good-Morning Stories

This next tradition is a wonderful adaptation of an old tradition to a new life-style.

Some traditions are so widespread, so commonplace, that we follow them automatically. We hardly think, for example, of reading a bedtime story as family tradition. "After all," says my friend Maria, "what kind of parent doesn't read her kid a bedtime story? So night after night I was reading to Danny through clenched teeth."

Danny is a terrific four-year-old. Adopted in Colombia when he was eight months old, he is an enchanting blend of sparkly hellion and solemn thinker. Unfortunately, shortly after his arrival, his father decided family life was too demanding and made abrupt goodbyes.

Maria was an ex-reporter who had been doing freelance writing since Danny's arrival. Through a combination of determination, skill, and luck, she landed a coveted job as a reporter for the morning newspaper. She loves the work, but the pay is poor and the hours worse. Her hardest time of day is battling traffic to Danny's day-care center before it closes at 6 p.m.

"By the time we get home, make dinner, talk a little, open the mail, and have a bath, it is Danny's bedtime. Usually, it is past Danny's bedtime. He is exhausted and cranky and so am I. And then we would need to read. I knew I was in trouble when I found myself hiding the long books."

That is when Maria and Danny came up with their own special tradition: good-morning stories. "Before Danny goes to bed," explains Maria, "we pick out our good-morning book. As soon as we are dressed and breakfast is on the table, we read. We usually talk about the story, or the ideas it triggers, in the car on the way to school. If the story is long or we get involved in talking and I am a little late, it is not so terrible. I blame it on the traffic. At least it is not the $1-a-minute late penalty that the day-care center charges in the evening.

"I am a more patient mother in the morning, and reading together is a pleasurable way for each of us to begin the day. Although this is not a tradition likely to continue through the years just as it is—I doubt that I'll be reading to Danny as a teenager—I really think it is establishing a basis for breakfast time as our time. Should Danny—perish the thought—ever turn into one of those head-in-shoulders, eyes-on-feet, muttering fifteen-year-olds, I'm betting breakfast will be our communication link."

Sin Night

This tradition was devised by a single parent to be a pressure valve in a very busy and structured family life.

Jane Winston is the poised and articulate headmistress of a posh girls' school. In earlier days, she was a single parent, teaching school and juggling her three children, bills, laundry, and the psychic needs of all the kids she taught. By Friday, there was not much energy left, and there were weekend chores and house-cleaning still to be done.

The Winston family response was to declare Friday night "off." The other six days of the week, everybody had to pitch in and help. Meals were balanced, kids were scheduled, parental commercials were delivered at regular intervals. On Sin Night, anybody could, within the bounds of reason, do anything he or she wanted, including Mom.

Nothing had to happen. You could eat or not eat; you could nibble with your fingers or dine on junk food. You could watch sex and violence on television, and go to bed without brushing your teeth. For one night, Supermom was off duty. She was not responsible for making dinner or cleaning up or supervising children.

It was every person for him- or herself, and the only rule was you had to clean up the kitchen after you cooked. The children could have overnight guests as long as their parents understood about Sin Night. Friends vied for a Friday-night invitation.

Nobody's teeth rotted on the spot, nobody's mind was irretrievably corrupted, and no one ever carried on so badly that serious repentance was required. Sin Night provided an excellent tension release in an otherwise pressured and tightly ordered existence.

The next two traditions deal with a particularly difficult time for single mothers, Mother's Day. I have not encountered single fathers who have anything similar, but a Father's Day picnic seems a perfect way for divorced or widowed dads to spend this day with their children. The ideas, of course, fit any holiday equally well.

Mother's Day / Father's Day Picnic

"If you don't have a sense of humor and good friends, you can get very depressed," says Nancy, the single mother of two small children. She and a friend annually organize the Unwed Mothers and Others Mother's Day Picnic to prevent Mother's Day depression.

It's a fluid affair. Friends are invited, and they are welcome to invite others. Somehow enough of a count is obtained to order from Kentucky Fried Chicken. Each person brings a dish and a beverage.

They meet in a suburban park, too small for anyone not to

find the group. The women play tennis and badminton and share in watching the children, who whoop it up in the sand-covered tot lot and come home sticky, gritty, and ready to fall into bed—just the way a good picnic should be.

"This year's picnic was such a success again that we decided to reassemble for our First Annual Father's Day Picnic," explained one mother.

"You and I know the world is full of divorced parents. But my daughter still has trouble understanding why we don't have a daddy in our house. These kinds of celebrations with other families in similar circumstances help me explain concretely that lots of people are like us. And they help me, too, because family days can be hard for me as well."

Reading Aloud

"I don't know what to say to my children when I have not seen them for a long time," thirty-eight-year-old Keith Muller admits. He is divorced and lives 150 miles away from his children. "It was awkward for us to get started. I wanted to be with them and have a sense of closeness, but I found it hard to figure out how to make it happen." Keith hit on a solution that eased his difficulties and opened the door to easier and more natural conversations. He reads.

Each holiday or summer visit, there is a book, carefully chosen, ready and waiting. On the very first evening, the reading begins. "Reading gives us all something to do and it casts a spell on us that we so very much need. I stop after the first chapter or two and ask them if they like the book, and this always works as a way to get us talking. If you read good books, not just junk, they are full of intense feelings, which make it easier for me to talk about my own feelings."

When the children were little, I read *The Velveteen Rabbit* and then the one about the mouse who is stranded on the island (*Abel's Island*). Then we read Roald Dahl books. *Danny, Champion of the World*, and *The Fantastic Mr. Fox* are great books to read aloud. The children's librarian also introduced me to the books of Madeleine L'Engle, and these are as much a joy for me to read aloud as for the children to listen to. This last vacation, we read Dickens. My son had to read one of his novels for class, and it was fun to read it together."

Do-It-Yourself Brunch

Mothers help to orchestrate Father's Day and fathers do Mother's Day. And single parents have a problem. These are the parents who most especially need a day in their honor, a day of being waited on and catered to. Without celebration, they can feel very glum.

After several years of uneventful, unceremonious, and glum Mother's Days, four single mothers got together and said, "Enough! We *need* Mother's Day, and if no one will give it to us, we will give it to ourselves."

They established their Mother's Day Brunch, which includes drawing names to buy presents and to help each other's children shop for a Mother's Day surprise.

"Organizing someone else's kids can be a bit of a pain when you're doing it, but the reward is worth it," explains one mom. "None of us has much of a family support system here and it is good for our kids to have the excitement of surprising Mom and even the involvement of working with another adult. Our children are all young. If we teach them now, hopefully they will learn to be thoughtful as they grow up."

The gifts the women buy for each other must be feminine

or frivolous. Pot holders, electric can openers, and child-rearing books are out. This year, lacy hose, a camisole, a gift certificate to Gourmet-to-Go, and a subscription to a woman's magazine were in.

The children give their gifts first and then are sated with apple juice and French toast and sent outside with an obliging baby-sitter. "We can usually come up with a sitter on Mother's Day by paying outrageously. If not, we abandon all semblance of responsible parenting and turn on the television."

Whoever is hostess cooks brunch so the other three get to play Queen for a Day—at least until it's time to help with the dishes. "We eat well, sip champagne, open our presents, and keep gloomy clouds at bay."

Birthday Potluck

Friends are important for all of us, but they are especially important to the single parent who has little or no family for support. Barb Freeman's potluck tradition focuses on birthdays, but like the above traditions it is easily applied to any event. In lieu of family, this birthday potluck supper with friends becomes the special celebration.

"My ex-husband's divorce decree specifies that he be present at the children's birthday parties," says Barb Freeman. "The first year I thought, Okay, what happens when all the guests go home and it's still the child's birthday and there the two of us are, standing in the kitchen . . . It seemed like more than I could handle, so I scheduled the children's party from three to five and invited some of the parents and some other friends to come at five for a potluck supper. That was how we began, and we have been having birthday potlucks ever since, for each of the girls' birthdays and for mine, too. I'm a Chinese-food addict, so we have Chinese potluck for me.

"It's fun. People are terrific about bringing good food and cleaning up and making it a real family-like celebration. It is actually more fun this way than it was with either of our families. That is one reason I didn't move back home after the divorce. My daughters are learning to celebrate with laughter and joy and song instead of ironed linens and good manners."

The At-Home Vacation

Another difficult time is vacation. Often there is a great need to get away and no money with which to do so. This is one solution.

Mattie Warrington is director of nursing for a busy St. Louis hospital. She is a soft-spoken, attractive black woman who conveys a sense of authority and competence. Like me, she has two boys, and we found ourselves comparing working-mother notes. "I think it has been easier for me to integrate family and work because I have always worked full-time. Neither I nor my family has known anything else. It seems to me that women who reenter the work force after having been at home full-time have the hardest adjustment," Mattie noted.

Mattie insisted their only important family tradition was eating out a lot. Restaurants are, she says, cheaper then psychiatrists. In fact, the Warringtons do have a long-established family tradition that started six years ago out of a need to be cheap but has persisted for pleasure. "Every summer we take a St. Louis vacation. We take three days and pretend we are tourists. Our boundaries keep expanding and sometimes we stay overnight in a motel. This year we are going to drive up to Springfield and do Lincoln County—stay overnight—but there are lots of things we've done just in the city. It's surprising how many things you never do when you live somewhere that you'd never miss if you came from out of town.

"For several years, it was the only vacation I could afford. Now we sometimes take away vacations, but we always have our St. Louis vacation, too."

Another single mother had a variation on this theme. She and her son take an "away vacation" by going to another part of town after work on a Friday and checking into a motel for the weekend.

"A motel with a swimming pool in another part of the city can be as much of an adventure for a young child as a trip away."

Wednesday-Morning Pancakes

Here is how a single mom makes time alone with each son.

Alice Burchard is 5' 1", about one hundred pounds, with curly, unruly hair and sparkly brown eyes. She looks like a college student. In truth, she's twenty-nine, widowed mother of Devon, seven, and Brett, eight and a half, and she sells office equipment that weighs more than she does.

Like single parents everywhere, Alice feels slightly breathless a good deal of the time. "There is never enough time. I thought money would be the issue, but it's not, it is time. A real problem for me is giving individual attention to each child. Since the boys are so close in age, there is a lot of competition and normal sibling rivalry. Normally, parents can divide and conquer on the weekends, but as a single parent that is seldom possible. At bedtime, I limit each boy to ten minutes with me. Otherwise, they would never get to bed, and I would never unwind. My solution is breakfast.

"Every Wednesday, I drop one boy at school early and take

the other to the pancake house. I don't try to force the kids to talk—at least I don't anymore, because it doesn't work. Sometimes Brett will read his *Electric Company Magazine* while I read the newspaper or we will do a kid's crossword puzzle together. But they know, every other Wednesday morning, I am theirs without competition or interruption.

"It makes me feel like a better mother, and I know it is important to the boys because they tell me Wednesday is the best day in the week."

7

Daddy Traditions

I N A LIBERATED WORLD, would there be a chapter of daddy traditions? What a glorious concept, to share the task of parenting equally. Adults and children would benefit together. But it
does not fit into most people's everyday realities, certainly not
mine. One of the things that most pleases me about my husband is his relationship with our sons. He cares; he worries; he
loves hard. And he works a lot. He is away from home far more
than I.

During our Seattle summer, Mike, intent on learning new
techniques to the point of mastery, spent seventy hours a week
in the lab. He missed spending time with the family but was
driven by the demands—and satisfactions—of work. I sat at the
dining-room table, writing and directing traffic. Our then eight-
year-old cuddled up to his daddy one night and said, "Daddy, I
love you, but I don't know you as well as Mommy."

In many households, one parent bears a disproportionate
responsibility for child-rearing. Usually it is Mom. These daddy
traditions come from men wanting to compensate for their absences, wanting to know their children and have their children
know them intimately.

Breakfast with Father

Peter Grazer is a hardworking lawyer, a partner in a downtown law firm where sixty- and seventy-hour weeks are normal. The Grazers have three children, now five, seven, and nine. About two years ago, Peter instituted what quickly became a cherished, inviolate tradition, father-and-child Sunday-morning breakfast.

Peter explained his catalyst: "Like a lot of guys, I work hard, but I'm also a family man. I began to feel alienated from my family. My wife knew the kids much better than I did! I worried about my relationships with them. I don't drive car pool or spend a Tuesday afternoon walking to the library or go on the class field trips. We try to spend as much time together as a family as we can, but with three young kids it is often a chaotic time. I can't cut back on my work hours, but I felt I was missing out on family stuff."

Peter began taking a different child out to breakfast each Sunday morning. They go most often to a local hotel, a favorite businessman's breakfast place during the week. It is a grownup kind of place where the coffee is good and the service is competent but not so fast that breakfast is over in ten minutes.

"The kids always know whose turn it is, and they obviously look forward to their morning. Frankly, I am more patient dealing with each child singly than I am juggling the whole crew at the end of a long day. I like unraveling and exploring the differences in each of our children. I find them amazingly good company over breakfast."

Their mother claims there is a happy side benefit. "When we eat out as a family, it is usually in fast-food places. This spring vacation I drove home to visit my parents without Peter and discovered the kids have learned real restaurant manners. They know about waiting for food, making quiet conversation, and tipping. Taking one child to grownup breakfast rather than three to grownup dinner is a much more economical way to teach restaurant manners, and it was a pleasant surprise."

The real payoff, of course, is not in better table manners. "I feel much better, much stronger about my relationship with the children now," says Peter. "It has made me want to spend more time with the children, be more involved in their activities, not because I think I should, but because I want to do it."

*

Throughout this book are variations on this special-breakfast theme. There is one in "Single-Parent Traditions" and a reference to something similar in one of the birthday traditions. Making designated meals special periods for individual children seems to work well in many families. Both parents and children speak with pleasure of such traditions. In one family, a father takes his daughters to dinner alone; in another, it is the mother and the teenage daughter who go off to dinner. In a third, it is grandparents who take the children to special weekly dinners.

The Daddy Book

Meals do not work if the parent is out of town. Here is a way to keep a traveling parent in touch with the everyday events of family life.

Over the last fourteen months, Carl Bruxton has come to dislike regular travel intensely. He has been spending three weeks of every month away from his family from Monday to Friday. For a bona-fide family man whose idea of a great day is to paint the porch and play a mini-version of touch football with Julie, seven, and Andy, nine, it has been very stressful.

Carl works for an Indianapolis-based company that acquired

a related business in Cleveland. The business had troubles, and Carl was given the tasks of fixing it and selling it. Both turned out to be more complicated than anyone anticipated and Carl became a reluctant commuter.

The work is interesting, but Carl misses being plugged into his family's daily life. The kids' accomplishments, defeats, treasures, and trivia from the week cannot all be neatly accumulated for Saturday-morning breakfast. Events, stories, and successes get misplaced and never shared.

Calling home helps, but frequently Carl is in meetings or entertaining and cannot call home with a sense of relaxation until the kids are in bed. Carl's traveling also made his wife, Jody, angry. She felt cheated and felt the kids were cheated. There was no point in yelling at Carl, because it made him miserable, too. Instead, she came up with the Daddy Book.

Most nights, after dinner, she and the children wrote down the important things of the day, the questions, the pleasures, the gripes, the feelings.

"Daddy, I wish you were home because Mommy is dumb about bicycles and I can't wait until Friday for you to fix my chain, and I don't think it is fair that you are gone so much," writes Andy. "I one my socker game today and scord a gole," writes Julie.

Sometimes they draw pictures or make up silly poems:

> *If you were here and we were there,*
> *Then we'd be bald and you'd have hair*
> *And you could come to the class play*
> *And we could sell your plant right away.*

"It is a time to be with Carl, if not in fact at least in spirit," says Jody. And when Carl comes home Friday night, the Daddy Book is always waiting to fill him in on all he has missed.

The Daddy Book is a very adaptable concept. It can be a Mommy Book or a Grandparent Book, too. It is, as a divorced father pointed out, a wonderful way for a weekend parent to keep in touch. And the Daddy Book need not only be child to adult. Daddies, or granddaddies or mommies, aunts or cousins can keep a book to share their lives, too.

Dad's Trip

Howard Jepson loves his cowboy boots, his jeep, and his weekend ranch. His wife, Ellen, found a snake in her bed at the ranch four years ago and has not been back since. Ellen, who is urban right down to her bright red toenails, does not miss the ranch and refuses to join Howard in other earthly delights like camping out, hiking, and rock climbing. Instead, Howard does these with his children. Each year, they have Dad's Trip, a week or so of outdoor activity that Howard plans with and for his kids.

"These trips," Ellen says, "came about not from any wisdom about parenting but from Howard's need to camp and have company. However, they have served another purpose as well. They change the family dynamics. It is the way the children have become close to their father and have learned to share feelings with him as well as me. It doesn't have to be camping. I just recommend father-and-child adventures of any sort."

First Day / Last Day

This tradition comes from a daddy who leaves most of the conventional holiday planning to others but has established his own special rite-of-passage celebration for the beginning and end of each school year.

New Traditions

The school calendar has irrevocably patterned my measure of time. My new year begins with Labor Day and takes a bend in time in June. Long after I was out of school and before we had children to replicate the routine, my psyche stayed tied to the first and last day of school emotions.

Wally Renko gives explicit recognition to these passages for his children. The first day of every school year is First Day Breakfast, a ritual that Wally orchestrates to marching music on the stereo. Wally cooks an elaborate breakfast. "It might be waffles with whipped cream and fresh strawberries or fried country ham and potatoes or Eggs Benedict or whatever captures my imagination, but it will not be the usual scrambled eggs and toast. This breakfast, after all, fortifies you for nine months of hard work."

The last day of school is celebrated with a small gift for each child, delivered over a German chocolate cake. "The gifts," says Wally, "are not a reward for performance, although excellent achievement does influence me. They are markers of accomplishment. Two of our children are collectors. Eric collects turtles and Gina collects stamps and usually their gift relates to their collection. Eric can give you a school history for half the turtles in his collection. Dick, our eldest, has more eclectic tastes and taxes my imagination a little more."

"Our kids," says Jean Renko, "would not miss that First-Day Breakfast or Last-Day Dessert for anything. Even the teenagers, and now we have two, put cynicism aside on these occasions. I attribute that to Wally, who is so absolutely serious about this, so committed to it. I probably would have been on-again, off-again about it, but this is Wally's thing. He does it with zest every year. I'm sure it is something our children will remember vividly as adults."

✳

Daddy Traditions

While food is an important ingredient in the Renkos' scheme, it is not essential. Plain old scrambled eggs and toast could be served on silver, in bed, to hard rock, with balloons. Served on everyday kitchen plates by a father who is, every other morning, gone before breakfast, the eggs become extra special.

Literary fathers can write poems, musical ones can compose songs, and funny daddies can concoct limericks or ridiculous stories. The concept embraces far more than back-to-school. Choose any event or any day it seems fun to bestow with daddy tradition: St. Patrick's Day, Halloween, the opening of the baseball season, Martin Luther King's birthday, the first day of spring, or the third Thursday in May.

8

Second-Stage Traditions

As I TALKED with families at different stages and ages, I came to the notion of second-stage traditions. When the children are growing up and the family is together in one house, first-stage traditions flourish. These are the traditions that shape and define the family, that form the memory patchworks we take into adulthood.

But as children go off to college or out into the world, first-stage traditions break down. The family that always and forever went out to dinner on Wednesday night to catch up with each other cannot do that when people are dispersed. Conflicting schedules, conflicting needs, and travel costs become factors to contend with. People not only move away physically, they spend time in different places emotionally, and family members feel out of touch with one another. Visits home are full of pulls between family and friends. A sense of separation can sit like a cloud through an entire visit.

As families grow up and disperse, first-stage traditions must give way to second-stage traditions, ways of maintaining family closeness and communication across distances.

Reentry

The Kunkels have been moving into the second stage slowly. A year ago, their family cup was used to toast the last of three children off to college. This year, the first year all three have been gone, Brett and Martha formalized a tradition that had been gestating with them. The second night that everybody is home is Kunkel Family Council Night, a time for talking together, for catching up, for reentering the family unit. In turn, each person talks about the best things that happened as a result of being away and the thing that each person missed the most. The parents talk about their year similarly. They then go around the family again and each person talks about something that bothered him or her that the family might share in. These subjects are left on the table for future conversations. In closing, each person shares something about his or her need to be with family.

"That took a long time, a couple of hours," Martha Kunkel said, "but we really felt at the end that we knew something of where each of us had been and each person had a time to say what was on his or her mind."

Goodbye Blessings

The above tradition is about coming home. In *The Second Jewish Catalog*, Sharon and Michael Strassfeld suggest we have a tradition for times when we must leave home. As I have gotten older and seen more children leave for college, travel, the military, or other adventures, I sense their push-pull feelings. They are often eager to be gone, to be out starting their own lives. But at the same time they are frightened and embarrassed to admit their anxieties.

I have not found a family that has a going-out tradition, but I like the notion. My nephew Andy has a group of friends from summer camp in Vermont who share a bell tradition. Each time they visit, a different person receives a little cowbell on a necklace. Whoever has the bell is responsible for finding a time soon to pass the bell on again. I like the idea that we give a child who is going out something special to hold on to. My practical son suggests I could reach out and touch him by giving him a telephone credit card. But what comes to my mind is a geode, those rocks that started off undistinguished but under the press of time and weight became full of glittering facets.

The Strassfelds also suggest a family moment in which the person who is leaving is blessed by the parents: "May the Lord bless you and keep you in your coming out and your going in. May the face of the Lord shine upon you and be gracious unto you." Those, or other, personal, words might be spoken at a family going-away dinner or at breakfast before each departure. Words do not give us strength, but the power of caring and commitment that words can convey do, I think, make us feel stronger and braver.

The Christmas Fund

Because my own family is so dispersed, I felt a kinship with the O'Donnells when they talked about their desire to maintain a sense of close family in the face of geographical distance.

The O'Donnells, two brothers and two sisters, grew up in Michigan outside of Detroit. Now their ages range from twenty-nine to thirty-seven. All are married with families and among them there are now nine children. The oldest brother, Sam, still lives in Michigan. Paul is a lawyer in Ohio. Megan lives in Washington, D. C., and Peggy, the youngest, ended up in New Orleans.

They came from a large extended family that had always had noisy, multi-generational family gatherings with lots of food and song and laughter.

Meg O'Donnell explains how they dealt with the breakup of this tradition. "My oldest brother, Sam, had kids first. Eventually, the family house got too big for our parents, and they moved out and Sam moved in, so we all just kept going home for Christmas. But as the rest of us settled down, had babies, and bought houses, we wanted to put roots down where we were living. I wanted my house to be a family home, too, and so did Paul and Peggy. And then Peggy always ended up with the biggest plane bills, which didn't seem fair. I don't know how it actually evolved, but one Christmas we just fell into the idea of a Christmas fund.

"Peggy is treasurer and each of us sends her $30 a month. This gives us about $1,500 every Christmas. That's our family travel money. And we rotate among ourselves hosting the others. Actually, although it is called the Christmas fund, we don't come together for Christmas anymore. We found that lugging the presents and not being home for Christmas morning wasn't great. Now we come together for four days around New Year's, and this is perfect. It is long enough to justify spending the money or driving a long way. It is short enough to keep us from getting on each other's nerves.

"The kids get to know all their cousins, aunts, and uncles; each of us gets a chance to have her home be the gathering place; the kids see some of the world; and no one has to bear the brunt of organizing two years in a row. Now some of the adults stay in a hotel, but the kids are all at the house. Over the years, we have sort of taken on special responsibilities. Paul and Peggy's husband always cook a gourmet New Year's dinner; I always organize an art project or contest for the kids; Sam and his oldest son make sure we have an outdoor challenge of some sort. Paul's wife is a morning person so she is permanent breakfast supervisor. Obviously, with a zillion people together, things sometimes fall apart, but everybody works hard to make it work because it is so important to us.

"The Christmas fund means no one has an unfair financial burden. It does not always get divided equally. If someone is driving and Peggy is flying from New Orleans, she would get a larger chunk. And now, with older kids and plane fares so high, it does not always cover the whole cost, but it means no one has to stay home or feel so worried about the expense."

The O'Donnells are a close family who appear extraordinarily flexible about dividing money or even trading host locations to adjust to particular needs. I suppose in some families this tradition could produce some tensions unless there were clear expectations, but, on balance, it seems to offer a very sensible way of funding the high cost of togetherness.

A Chair for the Missing

As the O'Donnells discovered, it is hard to get everyone home for holidays. The Molinas have three children who are always in various stages of coming and going. Since it has been rare, these past few years, to get everyone together at one time, they put a place at the table for those who are absent. "It is our way of saying that no matter where our children may be in body, in spirit they are in our hearts and in our minds, with us at the table."

St. Nicholas Lives

My extraordinary typist, Nancy Giljum, began typing for me while I was in Seattle. She and I had met only once before I left St. Louis for our Seattle summer, and I had no idea then of my good fortune in finding her until she returned the results of her wondrous word-processing machine with the following letter, which describes how a cherished childhood tradition is passed on by one enchanted adult.

"Reading of second-stage traditions reminded me of a very funny thing that happened to my brother as he was carrying out his St. Nicholas act.

"When we were children [of a Polish father] it was always a tradition to hang your stocking up on the eve of St. Nicholas [December 5] and wake up the next morning to find it full of goodies. Well, we are all grown up and away from home now, so my oldest brother, Jim, took it upon himself to continue the tradition in a slightly different way. Each St. Nicholas Eve, he gathers all kinds of goodies (candy, fruit, little games, and whatnot) and fills up huge mesh stockings. He then waits until about midnight and stealthily visits each of our homes, leaving a stocking for each of our children. Since it is outside the door the next morning, the children are certain their parents didn't do it and the younger ones really believe there is a St. Nicholas. It is certainly more credible than a Santa Claus coming down your chimney. We are wise to his game now and after the children are asleep, we always leave a little refreshment on our front doorsteps because our houses are from one end of the city to the other and that's a hard night's work for anybody.

"The funniest part, however, was last December 5, when my brother deposited three large stockings on our front doorstep (one for the baby and one each for my two stepsons). As he was creeping away to his car parked down the street, he was met by a Ladue policeman who wanted to know what in the world he was up to. My brother, so wrapped up in his game, told the policeman he was St. Nicholas. As Jim related later, it's a good thing our house was not his last stop because he had to show the policeman the car full of mesh stockings and explain his mission. He said that, had it been his last stop, no telling where he would have spent the night."

The Family Letters

Mary Maureen McCoullagh Riley says, with a name like that, it's no wonder she has six children. All of them have scattered, and to keep them in touch not only with her but with one another, Mary Riley has organized a practical second-stage tradition. She writes to her oldest, who adds a letter and sends it onto the next-oldest child. As the letters make their way around the family, each person receives six letters. The rule is that you should not hold the letter for more than ten days. With time in between for postal delivery, it means a turn at letter writing only about once a quarter. "The immediate news may be stale, but it gives us a feel for each other and it connects all of us directly without exorbitant phone bills."

The Postcard Connection

Sometimes just a postcard helps keep families in touch.

Her full name is Rosita O'Malley Goldberg, and her need for contact with her grandchildren—her *"wonderful* grandchildren," as she is quick to point out—will be understood by mothers and grandmothers everywhere.

Mama Rosita, as the family calls her, lives in Florida, but her five grandchildren are spread across the country: in Brooklyn, New York; Evanston, Illinois; and Colorado Springs, Colorado. Under these circumstances, holidays are difficult. "Thanksgiving should be a family time with everybody around one big table," says Mama Rosita. "Instead, we are apart."

Out of Mama's longing for a closer relationship with her grandchildren came this postcard idea. "All children love getting mail and, of course, they don't get very much. Unfortunately, I don't have the patience to write letters; I do send greeting cards, but they're not personal enough. It's easy to pick up the telephone, but phone conversations with kids don't always work. Then I hit on postcards.

"Wherever I am, I pick up cards. Sometimes I buy them; often I find them free. I always carry a stack and use them to send quick notes to the grandchildren.

"My grandson in Brooklyn loves hamburgers and chocolate shakes. So if I'm out to lunch, I'll write: 'Dear Jim, I'm sitting here eating a juicy cheeseburger and it makes me think of you. Can't wait to see you again. Until I do, chocolate milk shakes, chocolate hugs. Love, Grandma.' Or I'll find a funny postcard of a fat turkey and write, 'Huggles and Snuggles from Grandma,' and send it off to my Annie, who is four. Even if they don't see me for six months, the postcards let them know they're in my thoughts, so when we are together, there's a special bond between us."

One evening while visiting friends, I met a woman recently widowed. She was struggling hard to handle the changes in her life gracefully, struggling to hide the searing pain. She told me she had three grown children, one who worked on the West Coast, one in graduate school in another Midwestern city, and one at college nearby. None was married. "I have talked with them," she said, "about coming home periodically, coming back for us to spend time together." It was not working out so well. "The children's schedules conflict or they seem reluctant. When they are home, they are so busy seeing old friends, the time passes too quickly."

Uncomfortable memories stirred inside me. I thought of visits I had made home, visits sometimes made reluctantly, visits so overscheduled with relatives and friends that adults as well as children got cranky. I thought more happily of the one weekend I had decided to fly home alone only to see my mother. We had a lovely time, two adults having lunch, browsing in shops, enjoying each other.

I thought, too, of a letter to Ann Landers that prompted my husband to end a business trip by stopping in Pittsburgh just to take his mother to dinner. This letter was written by a woman who said she loved her daughter-in-law and was grateful to her for the calls and cards and gifts, but that it would be nice to hear from her son occasionally.

There is this betwixt-and-between time when children are no longer children but are not yet quite settled as adults—a post-childhood, pre-parent stage when "going home" may lose its magic. As we struggle to grow from child to adult, the habitual childhood roles that home so often triggers can irritate us. Our lives are not at home any longer, yet our families seem hardly impressed by the new adults we feel we have become. In these years when we are ready to put down our roots but still are anxious about how well we will do, we want reassurance. And the reassurance may come not by going home to the comforts of childhood but by beginning to integrate those comforts into our own new physical spaces and emotional places.

This strong desire to build nests of our own, to assert our own rhythms and patterns is healthy. If it creates tensions, those tensions might be viewed as positive spin-offs of strong family feelings in people who no longer live under one roof and are each pulling toward a different home base.

I wondered if the widow who triggered these thoughts of mine might need to put off family gatherings at her house for some years and substitute floating reunions distributed among the places where her children live. Her children needed a chance to show her and to show each other who they were in their own contexts. They needed to reassure her visibly that they, too, were going to survive this wrenching loss.

Do you remember the pride you took in your first apartment? I was so pleased with mine, with my clever decorating with other people's leftovers. I liked having my parents to dinner, liked showing them how well I had learned to cook, how gracious a hostess I was, how grownup I had become.

When children begin to make their own homes, part of second-stage traditions is allowing, encouraging, and rewarding those impulses. Sometimes parents need to "go home" to their children, even if home is not very commodious or well appointed.

My neighbors got through their children's prickly twenties with an enviable tradition. It is the most expensive one in this book, but I include it because it works so well for children who are scattered and have trouble coming home to cohabit again. Each Christmas, my neighbors invite all their children—three married daughters and a son still in school—with spouses and offspring to be guests at a fancy resort. Each couple has a cottage for retreating. No one needs to take a turn with the dishes. There is plenty to do, and it is easy to do it together. No one of them can resist the lure of a lovely free vacation, and the parents have maximum family time with minimum friction.

In your own family, the siblings may have chosen very different life-styles. One may be settled in the suburbs with kids and house and dogs. Another may be a single in a city high-rise with an expansive view and a minuscule kitchen, or a graduate student crammed into married-student housing, or a starving artist sharing a house with other starving artists.

If the single city dweller is delighted to escape a 6' x 8' kitchen and head for the suburbs to celebrate, terrific. Just be sure he or she is not secretly wishing a more central role. This apartment might not be the place to which you rotate Thanksgiving dinner, but it might be fun for a nieces-and-nephews slumber party with a post-party family brunch. A corner of someone's campus is perfect for picnics, and all the starving artists I know do pumpkin carvings and chili dinners with panache.

Our need for family ties and our ability to create new traditions does not depend on whether we own dining-room chairs and china cups or whether we have children. And if our second stages are only preludes to still other stages, only transitional times, then we must fit our traditions to these transitions.

9

When There Is Just You

I N AN EARLIER VERSION of this book, I focused on couples and single parents, but I overlooked single adults—a growing group that deserves its own new traditions. I think my neglect signified a tendency to discount the requirements of single people or to assume that they will simply be included in the activities of the couples' world. Many of the traditions elsewhere in this book will work for single people, but single people have singular needs.

I started out thinking of a single adult as a family of one. My interviewees said no, one is not a family. But family was a recurring theme in the interviews. Some people spoke of inventing ways to escape the ongoing demands of their primary family. "As the only single daughter in a family with four married siblings, you have to do this and you have to do that because you have more time . . . I do a lot of favors for the others, but it doesn't seem that many favors are done for me. I am envious of the single men I know who travel over their holidays," complains a corporate executive in California who lives in close proximity to her entire family.

Other people regretted that their families were too far away geographically, too removed emotionally, or too dispersed, with no magnetic core to reassemble the clan. Whether as counterpoint to constant family pressures or to fill in the blanks in the absence of family, the desire for a supportive group of caring people shaped many of the new traditions of single people.

Turf Time

Jane Taylor, a thirty-nine-year-old training director with a large engineering company, says the message she gets from her family, unintended perhaps, but distinct, is that you only count if you have a house and some children: "For all these years, I had gone 'home' to Toledo, where my parents live, or Phoenix, where my married brothers live. Never had my family come, en masse, to Houston, where I live. Suddenly that didn't feel right anymore. I announced that I needed a gathering of the clan on my turf. My family had a zillion reasons why that wasn't a good idea. At first, I felt hurt. Then I sort of understood that they weren't trying to be mean. They just didn't understand. I held my ground, and this past Thanksgiving, everyone came here. I think having them all together in my world, in my condo, in my office, and having me clearly be the hostess finally helped my family to perceive me as a grownup. And we all had a great time. From now on, every now and then, the celebrations will be on my turf."

Singles Hour

Dora Daniels is a forty-three-year-old big-city magazine editor who enjoys visiting her large and close-knit family in the small Virginia town where she grew up. "But I have to think carefully about how to structure the relationship so as not to be sucked in as a minor player. In order to keep going home for holidays, I need to make sure some of my own needs get met." Her solution has been to gather the single adults of her generation together. "This chance for us, the 'older children' as we are thought of, to have our own time to talk about our own issues has been surprisingly wonderful for all of us. It is such a simple thing and takes no more than a few hours, but it has changed the way I feel about these trips home. It has legitimized my feelings within the family context—and oddly enough, where, as a single single, there was a sense of wistfulness for me, as a group we seem to have a certain romantic quality."

Gift-of-Self

It isn't always better to give than to receive, but in giving, there can be a great deal of getting, say Scott Miller and Sandy Goldsmith. Sandy and Scott first became friends at All Saints Church, serving dinner to two hundred homeless people. This Thanksgiving, Sandy was at a day shelter in Roxbury helping to cook, serve, and clean up a hundred meals, and Scott scooped stuffing at a homeless shelter. "I don't enjoy the usual Thanksgiving feast," Sandy explains. "There is no appreciation and gratitude when you sit at a table filled with food, with nothing to remind us why we are there and what good fortune we have. Working in shelters on the holidays fills me with a deep sense of good fortune. It certainly keeps you from feeling sorry for yourself."

Peter Ware, a Midwestern patent attorney, spent his Christmas at the local Children's Hospital, cuddling babies recovering from their mothers' crack addiction. A group from the New York advertising world hold an annual Easter egg hunt for impoverished children, and residents of a singles apartment complex take over the game room to cook and serve a Mother's Day dinner to battered women and their children.

If the idea of making someone else's holiday more cheerful makes you feel happy, but you are not sure where to volunteer, try calling the Salvation Army, the Catholic diocese, the United Way volunteer coordinator, or an organization for the homeless in your community.

Adopt-a-Family

Lots of single people link up with married friends for holidays and special occasions. These get-togethers seem to cross the line from dinner to tradition when there is mutual benefit. Rod Westerman, a bachelor in his mid-thirties, has this kind of relationship with his college roommate's family. "What makes it really work is that I have long ago moved from being a visitor to being one of the family—which means I pitch in, instead of being waited on like a guest. I don't cook, and Sally is fussy about having the food just right, so I don't even offer to bring dishes anymore. But I traditionally send fabulous, extravagant flowers for the table, and they are really appreciated.

"I also take Greg and Sally out to a nice restaurant for their anniversary. They would be reluctant to spend the money themselves. When I think of all the times I would have been tempted to go out of town just to avoid being alone on a holiday, I figure they have saved me thousands of dollars, and it isn't so much to spring for a special dinner once a year."

A thirty-five-year-old executive secretary in Manhattan has a similar relationship with an old friend and the friend's husband. She flies to California every Christmas. "We pack up the car with more stuff than I can describe and meet Joe's parents at a dude ranch. I am an added ingredient, a different spice in the pot. I create levity. Joe's parents are stiff and structured, and I breathe life into the family; I'm a comedic influence. I can make fun of things that are taboo in the family. I bring good stories and neat presents. Last year, I couldn't go because I had my appendix out, and Peg called and said, 'I could almost hate you for not coming.' So I know they aren't just being nice to me, that I give something to them."

She reflects on couples-single relations in general: "I think single people, given the opportunity, are more interesting than the couples' world gives them credit for. When you are single and in your thirties or older, some people look at you as a failure. The American dream is to grow up and marry, and if you are not married or on the route to a married state, they look at you and say, 'Oh, you poor thing,' instead of 'Who are you?' "

Sometimes it's lonely, she says. "I would like to have dates, really have more friendships, but when the world looks at single females, it doesn't see how smart we are and how much we have to contribute and what interesting lives we lead. I am determined that mine will be a full life, and, for me, that means traditions."

Brunch Bunch

Some people hate being home on a Saturday night or not having a comfortable place to unwind after work on Friday. When I was single, I often found Sunday afternoons particularly lonely. I would have wanted to be part of the Brunch Bunch, twelve friends who host a rotating noon brunch each Sunday. Guests are always welcome, no apologies for missing, dress informal, newspaper reading allowed, atmosphere convivial. "One of the reasons this works," explains a member of the group, "is that early on we stopped trying to prove we could be 'hostess with the mostest.'

We like being in each other's houses because it is more informal and relaxed than a restaurant, but we don't worry about these brunches being gourmet deals. The food is fine, but there is no burden on you to do anything special—and that is why I think it has lasted for so many years. If someone opts out (over the years, people have moved, married, lost interest), someone new joins, so hosting is only a few times each year."

This camaraderie-cum-food has multiple variations for single people. In St. Louis, I uncovered the ROMEO Club, Retired Old Men Eating Out, which meets once a week in the city's best restaurants. For a group of single men in Dallas, it is beer and barbecue on Friday nights; for four young women in San Francisco, it is "stave off the Saturday-night blues" with Chinese food; and for singles in Boston, it is a regular pickup potluck. Regardless of the menu, all these people find that having a defined time to get together beats ad hoc scheduling. "It is much easier and better for my mental health," says a hardworking twenty-four-year-old Boston paralegal, "to cancel if it doesn't work one week than to have the continual burden of trying to organize myself into scheduling something. And I find that even if I start out feeling blue, being with friends lifts my spirits."

Always at My House

Both young single people and people who have been married for decades and then widowed can have trouble thinking of themselves as solo hosts or hostesses. There are no rules about who can entertain. People who used to be couples should not stop entertaining when they stop being part of a couple. It only takes one gracious, welcoming host or hostess to make for a wonderful time.

Many people spoke of institutionalizing annual gatherings for various occasions. Amy Wang, a research librarian in Philadelphia, felt particularly passionate about her new tradition. "Every Thanksgiving, I used to go to the suburbs to visit some cousins I actually disliked. They always put me in a blue funk, but I went because I wanted tradition, I wanted to have that place you always go to for this or that occasion. One grim year, I said, 'No more.'"

Amy marched out to buy an expandable table with multiple leaves and flap-up sides that almost fills her apartment, and declared her house as the place to come for Thanksgiving. "It is my time to be matriarchal. Lots of people have nowhere to go and nothing to do on days when you want to be with people you care about. And this isn't only single people. But no one wants to admit they don't have anything to do. It makes you feel particularly unloved. Now both single and married friends know they are welcome at my house for potluck Thanksgiving. We read poems of thanksgiving, we sing, we laugh, and we eat well."

A few years ago, Amy added a Labor Day picnic just because she liked the idea of starting off the fall with something special and found that being in the park with a volleyball net, a battery-powered radio and tape deck, and a grill was an easy way for her to entertain a crowd.

A widow in an apartment house uses the common room for a Granny party around Christmas. Her friends are invited to come and bring their young grandchildren. A widower, grateful for all the dinner invitations of his friends but thoroughly intimidated by the thought of reciprocating on his own, arranges a theater party each year at a small local theater. After the performance, he hosts a reception in the lobby for his guests.

Matchmaking

Where there are single people, there is matchmaking. Some of the most inventive rituals, old and new, are stimulated by a matchmaker impulse. A group of New York parents watched with dismay the work-oriented lives of their successful but unmarried children. The younger generation was so involved in high-pressure, fast-paced careers that they had little opportunity to develop a social life. The parents decided to host a monthy Sunday at-home afternoon tea, and although at first the offspring ridiculed and resisted, these have turned out to be successful and agreeable events.

Three women in New York host an annual Valentine's Day party to which dozens of single women are invited. Each is asked to invite an available, uninvolved man or two.

On an airplane, my seatmate told me about his favorite restaurant, which on weekends has a large, round, singles table. People know they can come alone and be welcomed at the community table. He wondered what it would take to get more restaurants to start such a table, a big improvement, he found, over standing at a bar.

An art historian says her friends have a ritual around art openings. "We all go and everyone uses this as a time to meet new people and see old friends and catch up with gossip."

The Travel Habit

While many of us are braving the retail stores, wrapping gifts, and sweeping up pine needles or eggshells or birthday-cake crumbs, legions of people can be found sunning and skiing and exploring exotic corners of the world for holidays or birthdays or as annual summer retreats. A judge in San Francisco always spends the last two weeks of December in some remote location. He has gone skiing in Switzerland, scuba diving in the Caribbean, and animal watching in Africa. An accountant who loves horses plans a riding vacation each fall, most recently on the English moors. A wine connoisseur goes to France; and a health administrator meets her college roommate, now married and delighted to have some "just me" time, for a week of photography in a scenic spot.

Some people complained that they would like to travel more but can't find a travel companion. Mindy Berks, a college professor in Louisiana, had this problem, but decided against staying home. "One advantage of living alone is the opportunity to walk out the front door and take off for parts unknown, to throw a dart at the map and say, 'What the heck, let's go.' But I found it was impossible to find a traveling companion. My friends with enough spunk to be adventurous didn't have the money to take the kinds of trips I wanted. Those with the money didn't have the spirit. Or there were impossible scheduling problems. I have given up trying to coordinate my travel with others. I just go.

"At first, I worried about being lonely or becoming ill and having no support. I started subscribing to travel magazines and found group programs that worked for me, that had enough flexibility and variety of people to make me feel I wasn't part of a herd."

Berks admits to a few lonely moments but says they are substantially outnumbered by the wonderful times and memorable adventures. "My advice to people who want to do this is to do some research. There are so many different kinds of organized trips now that most everyone can find something suited to them." There are trips for singles, for families, for grandparents traveling with or without grandchildren, for bikers and hikers and shoppers, culture lovers of every art, and minimalists who want to think about Zen in Japan.

It is no longer possible to do Europe on $5 a day, but there are budget options for low-cost travel. Nan Fielding annually fills her backpack and joins one of the many hiking and camping trips sponsored by the Sierra Club. She loves the inclusive and friendly feeling of these groups. Ray Richman is addicted to the reasonably priced and stimulating programs organized by Elder Hostel for people sixty or older. Elder Hostel offers a catalogue full of educationally oriented programs at colleges and conference centers around the world. A San Francisco bachelor with a coveted bay-view apartment is working on establishing a new house-swapping tradition with the help of an international organization that brokers such exchanges. Stephen Ulling, who teaches second grade and has his summers off, has spent the last four summers traveling the world for free as the leader of teenage summer groups.

Family Vacation

Kim Mason had a different sort of travel problem. She was torn between her desire to spend holidays with her family and her equally strong desire to spend some of her scarce vacation time somewhere more exciting than Oklahoma City.

"I proposed that we make one holiday each year a family vacation away. I was really nervous about suggesting this. Finally, I got up my courage and popped it out, and I was stunned at how readily everyone else took to it. It turned out all the women in the family were delighted. They had been envying me for always arriving at the last minute, with none of the burdens of

preparation. This way, we still have a family holiday, only someone else does the dishes."

My Eyes Only

"I was buying a pumpkin just before Halloween with someone
from my office. 'Why do you want it?' he asked me. I told him I
wanted it for my house. 'Who is going to see it?' he said. What
do you mean, who is going to see it?" says Natalie Ortega, her
voice rising in indignation. "I'm going to see it!"

Ortega is a photographer and filmmaker who loves the
house she struggled to buy and fix up and feels strongly about
having it reflect her delight in traditions and holidays. "I refuse
to think of myself as wanting because I am single. Just because
I am alone is no reason to diminish my world. I am worth the
effort. It is enough that *I* live here and take pleasure in holiday
rituals and traditions." Ortega is intent on collecting holiday decorations from every country of the world.

Angelo Menotti has earned a neighborhood reputation for
his wreaths. Each holiday, a special and spectacular wreath dec-
orates his door. His friends have taken to giving him unusual
wreaths as gifts, and a wall in his dining room is hung with these
circular sculptures.

For Sally Johnson, it's teddy bears. Each bear holds the memory of a trip or a friend or a special event, and they all come out
of storage in December to be household company to Sally as she
celebrates her birthday on the eighth, as well as Christmas and
the New Year.

For each of these people, the impetus to decorate has intersected with the compulsion to collect. Holidays are a time to
share and savor their favorite collectibles.

Kids Only

Grandparents are meant to spoil children. So, it seems, according to many people with whom I have spoken, are single aunts and uncles. Neal McMurtey, a bearded, thirty-three-year-old landscaper, thinks it is important to be around children to keep the child inside himself alive and well. His nieces and nephews and young cousins pick up on this instantly and adore their Uncle Neal. Their affection for him is fed each Thanksgiving by Neal Night. While the grownups have dinner down the road with Neal's parents, Neal does his kids-only, no-turnips feast.

Janet Rotel forges connections among the next generation on Memorial Day. All the young people in the family, from eight to eighteen, come to a weekend pajama party at her apartment. "We eat junk food and go to the movies and bowling and roller skating and play charades and tell ghost stories, and I get to know these kids in a different way than when they are with their parents."

Julia Garez, one of ten brothers and sisters, has "a zillion" nieces and nephews. Garez, a nurse "in the middle years," offers these kids a bit of magic. Each spring vacation, she invites one or two of her young relatives on a trip. "At first, I took them to places I wanted to go. But I have gotten better at this over the years, and now I pick places that fit their interests. It's been wonderful for me. I have gone places and done things—like fly-fishing—I would never have done on my own.

"There is a selfish element in all this. I am not going to have kids of my own, and in my old age I want to know there will be people close to me who care about me. These trips are wonderland adventures for the kids; I am the fairy godmother. They tell me their secrets and their fears, and I tell them they are wonderful and powerful and dreams can come true."

Compensations

Loni Edwards lives only a few miles from her parents, but she, like David Redmond and Paul Spaymacker, never gets home to celebrate. All three are homosexuals in stable, committed relationships with people who are not welcomed by their parents.

"My parents have done a terrible thing," says Loni. "They have asked me to choose not only between them and the woman I love and live with but between their values and my values, between what is important to them and what is important to me. I can't describe the pain, but I will tell you that I refuse to live a lie, to pretend that I am their good little girl waiting for Prince Charming to sweep her off to the suburbs because this makes them happy. I would like nothing more than to have the same kind of large, family celebrations that we would have had if I had followed the traditional script.

"Since this is not possible, Ruth and David and Paul and I and some other people we know have invented our own family, and we are working on establishing our own traditions. We are committed to trying to become an extended family for each other, and we are trying to establish rituals that work for us. For the past several Christmases, we have gone caroling and then cooked an elegant dinner, with champagne. One gift tradition is books, and we compete to find the perfect book for each person. Ruth, the woman I live with, and I have another tradition. Since those of our family who accept us still spend the holidays with the nuclear family, we don't get to see them. So we host a New Year's Day open house for family and friends, and we give family members their gifts then."

Breakfast Club

Mary Keefe and Jan Paul and Randy Reasoner like to get up and talk to people in the morning. But they all live alone. So they meet, most weekday mornings, for breakfast at a diner. "It just keeps us in touch. Good friendships," explains Mary, "are like family relations; they aren't built on great ideas and profound insights but on dailiness, on sharing who said what to whom and how you broke your diet and how bitchy your boss is. That's what we talk about at breakfast."

Letter Writing

I get lots of mail every day, most of it junk or bills. It is seldom that I get a "real" letter, and I cherish these. Mostly, my friends and I stay in touch by phone, but a letter is qualitatively different. The act of writing it transforms my thinking, and reading it and rereading it makes the pleasure linger far longer than a phone conversation.

So when Barrie Edmonds told me about her favorite tradition, I felt a little envious. For twelve years, Barrie and François Campeau have exchanged letters once a month. Friends and colleagues more than a decade ago in Paris, they see each other seldom. Their correspondence is a compendium of their personal and professional lives. Although they are decades apart in age, both teach nineteenth-century French literature, share an interest in twentieth-century art, in music, and in observing cultural mores.

"This correspondence is the most intimate aspect of my life," says Barrie. "For each of us, the writing serves a very personal need to reflect, to introspect, and then to try to articulate what it feels like, knowing one won't be judged. Beyond the self-centeredness of it, we can write things to each other and hear each other's voice in ways we could never do face to face, day to day. And our age difference makes these letters all the more interesting."

There is something very Victorian about writing, and it seems a lovely counterpoint to lives in which we impatiently fax each other and get updates on the car phone. Perhaps it is the writer in me that so vividly imagines the pleasure of receiving letters as a teenager or a college student, the satisfaction of taking the time to write more often to old friends and dear relatives, and the delight of future generations when they come upon these letters.

The X and Y Problem

Having children is surely the first family tradition. This oldest tradition is being widely restructured today by single people in their thirties and forties who, though not married, are unwilling to forgo parenting.

Kay Damian was widowed in her thirties. Five years later, pessimistic about marrying again, she adopted a baby girl from India. Rebecca Golden, a thirty-seven-year-old rabbi, has joined a support group for single women planning pregnancies. "I would rather do this as a married woman, but I am not married, and the biological clock is ticking." She has investigated and found that artificial insemination in a local Boston hospital is both accessible and affordable. She is unsure what impact this will have on her professionally, but she is sure it is the right personal choice.

Both straight and gay men and women are, in increasing

numbers, becoming parents by birth or adoption. These families can be expected to be rich with new traditions because what they are doing is both extraordinarily traditional and extraordinarily new.

Nuclear Family Weekend

Seth, Susan, and Scott Semmens grew up with the usual sibling rivalries. But when their parents died, they found a strong bond linked them in deep affection. Seth and Susan are married, with children. Scott, the oldest, is single, and it was he who proposed the nuclear family weekend, a once-a-year expedition for just the three of them. "I love the kids, and I am good friends with Susan's husband and Seth's wife, but the family dynamics are different when we are all together. Frankly, I often feel outnumbered, or maybe emotionally outweighed. Anyway, these weekends have been really good for all of us. We can fight one-on-one, we can reminisce, we can catch up and get to know each other as grown-ups. Seth and Susan like the chance to escape the domestic chaos for a bit, and because it is family, their spouses are agreeable. In fact, Seth's wife has begun taking a similar weekend with her two sisters."

Birthday Reflection

"Do you do anything special for your birthday?" I always ask. Most people like to go out to dinner with friends or family. A few make an effort to schedule a weekend trip somewhere or to see old friends.

Jim Pappas, an agency art director who is just forty, has, over the past decade, gradually rejoined the Greek Orthodox Church of his childhood. It has provided him with community, with old traditions, and with an awakened sense of spirituality that is reflected in his birthday tradition.

"I love my birthday. I think everybody, at every age, should celebrate the birth day. I reflect on my birthday. I start in the morning, in bed, as soon as I remember it's my birthday. I stay there, thinking back on the year and how it's been. Then I get up and enjoy every minute of the day. I make it a day of heightened awareness. I try to look for beauty and for pleasure and for good in people. I use my birthday to renew my confidence in myself and in the future."

10

Giving Traditions

A CONGREGATIONAL MINISTER suggested that amid this celebration of family, there be some traditions focused outwardly, traditions where families gave of themselves to others. I liked his idea.

We say it is better to give than to receive, but most of us must be doubters, because giving traditions are even scarcer than anniversary traditions. Lots of people give of themselves as individuals, but hardly any of us have traditions—new or old—that involve giving as a family effort. Perhaps we give money, invite people who are lonely to share a meal, take cans to the food bank, or bring gifts for the poor to church. But so few of us give when it is difficult, when it requires meeting needs that in no way fit our own.

I am full of excuses for why my family does not do these things. There is so little time for us; we give money instead; what difference would my small gesture make. Yet little gestures offered to me have so much meaning—being invited to a family celebration when we are in a new place; a friend dropping off an interesting book; a co-worker going out of his way to make my job easier. And, in truth, my excuses sound shallow even to my own ears. I know we have so much good fortune, by the happenstance of fate. Were we less lucky, what would I wish from others?

Having thought all this, I found I was still not ready to say yes when we were asked to take responsibility for a family of immigrants or to give up our Thanksgiving to serve food to others. I looked for those people who were willing. What was interesting was that they were not turning up at all in the normal networking patterns I used. If I wrote about the exceptional people, I worried, would their ideas work for other families? It seemed important to find examples from people whose professional work did not lead them to helping.

We cannot expect our children to be giving, charitable adults by telling them to be so. We encode them with our own behaviors. The three new traditions in this section are here because they are examples of giving traditions from which all of us can learn and to which I think most of us can relate.

Lenten Giving

I thought I might find a tradition of giving to others at Christmas. Instead I found it at Easter in the home of a Presbyterian minister and a third-grade teacher, a home that has so consciously developed and fostered family traditions that there are three Kunkel traditions in this book. For this family, Lent is a time of giving, not giving up.

It is their Lent tradition that, instead of giving up something, each Kunkel gives something of himself. Every person in the family decides what he or she will give and to whom it will be given. It may be within the family, or it may involve others outside the family.

"This year," says Martha Kunkel, "I wrote a letter each day of Lent to someone we'd known and cared for but hadn't been in touch with recently. Actually, I didn't write every day, but over the Lenten period I did write twenty letters in all. I got either a phone call or a letter back from everyone. It was terrific. One of my daughters started a plant and took it to an elderly couple she used to work for and spent some time visiting with them. Last year, for example, we took an evening to have people to dinner that we care about and would like to know better but had never found time to invite. One of our daughters made a date with a girl in her class who was feeling unpopular and left out. Another year, the giving may focus more on family members, but each of us does give something of himself."

Any holiday, any day, can be a time for giving. I think most of us care about others, want to be kind and thoughtful, but we get too caught up in juggling our own lives. Making giving a tradition helps us remember how good it can feel to give and how little effort is often required to feel like a sunshine maker.

Most of the names in this book have been changed, but Tom Lickona is the real name of a psychology professor at the University of New York at Cortland. I met Tom when he came to St. Louis to talk about moral development in young children. We were both working on books, and his *Raising Good Children* had already been accepted for publication. Having found a kindred spirit, I was delighted when Tom offered to read my manuscript. He gave me sensitive criticism, important encouragement, and good advice. He also gave me the following tradition, which I leave in his words.

Fast Dinner

"I also wanted to share with you a family tradition that has much meaning for us. A senior colleague at the college teaches a course on world hunger. For many years, he has fasted on Monday of each week—liquids all day. He sends the money saved to an international organization that relieves hunger and famine around the world. His example inspired me to propose the following to the family: that on Monday night, we'd have a 'fast dinner' (sliced apples or oranges for the kids, broth and crackers for Judith and me). You know, as I write this, I realize I've got it wrong. It was actually my son, Matthew, who first proposed we do this after an appeal for Oxfam and fasting at the Boston University Chapel Mass we used to go to when we were there. That is, Matthew suggested we fast, and I told him what my friend John Willmer did, and we worked out a modified plan. Yes, that's it. Well, anyway, Matthew wrote a special prayer that we use for grace on that night:

> *Lord, we pray for all the hungry people in the world, that they may become well and fed, and that the pain they suffer will be lifted from their hearts—and that all people in the world will turn their hearts to generosity and compassion.*

"The money we save by not having a regular dinner we put in a glass jar. After a month or so, we send off what we have accumulated to Oxfam. Sometimes at dinner on these nights, we'll read a letter we've received from Oxfam reporting progress made in relieving hunger in one part of the world or the outbreak of a new crisis somewhere else. I see this as an important kind of consciousness raising for the kids, something that's consistent with our religious belief in love of neighbor. It's also a way of making real the idea that we are, all of us, one human family. And by depriving ourselves a little, we understand better the hunger of less fortunate people.

"I don't mean to exaggerate our 'sacrifice'; this tradition has had unexpected pleasant spin-offs. Judith likes the fact that she doesn't have to prepare dinner on the first day of the week; that gives her more of the day for things she'd like to get done. And we have a snack before bedtime to quiet our growling stomachs—usually tea and a muffin with jam or peanut butter. That Monday-night snack has become a time of togetherness for Judith and me (the boys have theirs sooner, then to bed). We talk about lots of things, big and small. And I find that on Monday night a near-empty stomach makes for an unusually clear mind—I get a lot accomplished after dinner!"

Tiny Volunteers

The third giving tradition is one I found in *Redbook* magazine, in a column called "A Young Mother's Story." There seemed no need to try to improve on the way its author, Lynn S. Rubin, had described this lovely new tradition.

"Last winter, during a spell of awful weather, Alan, my two-year-old son, grew restless from being cooped up in the house. To make matters worse, I was feeling sad because my grand-mother had recently died, and she had never seen him. Then I remembered a visit we had made to my husband's uncle in a nursing home while we were on vacation last summer.

"Alan had stayed in his great-uncle's room for about two minutes before he started toddling up and down the hall, in and out of other rooms, making animal noises and showing off as only a fifteen-month-old can. The patients were enchanted. Old women who had been staring at television or out the window were suddenly smiling and lively as they cooed at him and patted his head. One elderly man followed him down the hall, chuckling and calling to everyone he saw, 'Hey, come look at this!' By the time we left, patients who had been gazing vacantly into space were standing in the hall and talking to one another about 'that sweet baby.'

"Countless elderly people are in nursing homes. Many are far away from their families and many never see their grand-children, if they have them—or any other children, for that matter. And many children grow up without regular contact with an older generation. That's always bothered me, because there's something about the exchange between children and old people that's very special. So I put it all together and, after talking with a few friends, planned a play group.

"First I called the program director of the nearby Keswick Nursing Home. She set up a meeting with the director of volunteers to work out the details—this must have been the youngest group of volunteers they'd ever had!—and we were in business. We would meet every other week; each mother would stay with her child, of course, the entire time; and we would bring our own toys. The nursing home agreed to list us on its calendar of activities (we're officially called the Children's Hour), and any patients who wanted to could participate.

"We started on a miserable winter day with three children and about a dozen patients. The weather was so bad that the nursing-home staff and the patients weren't sure we would get there. No one knew what to expect, but we had decided that we would keep the Children's Hour very low-keyed and informal. We dumped our toys in the middle of the floor, and the patients, most of them in wheelchairs, formed a large circle around us. The two boys, Alan and Andrew, immediately ran into a corner to see the 'grandpa clock.' Meg, then seven months old, sat on the floor, sucking on her fist and occasionally crawling around a bit. The morning progressed and more patients dropped in to see what was going on, and the children warmed up as they got used to the room. With some encouragement they began to show their toys to the patients or chat for a moment, with a mommy/

interpreter close by. Alan and Andrew were fascinated with the wheelchairs. They called them 'funny tricycles' and laughed about the 'big fat tires.' They tried to send a motorized one for a ride (the patients soon learned it was advisable to disengage the gears as soon as they came in), and then tried to take one apart. The boys thought the wheelchairs were great, and it never occurred to them that there was the slightest thing unusual about the people in them. It didn't seem to matter if the patients couldn't hear or see very well, or walk or talk. It didn't matter if they had cerebral palsy or Alzheimer's disease or some other debilitating illness, or if they were just old. The children accepted the patients totally, and the feeling was definitely mutual. Perhaps the children were too young to be frightened or embarrassed. Older children who since have come to the group seem to need more preparation. They are more timid and will hang back, or point and say, 'What's wrong with her?' We try to be very matter-of-fact when that happens, and no one has ever been very upset. But the children who start coming to the group before they are about two years of age seem never to develop any fear of the patients or embarrassment, although they sometimes, naturally, do exhibit some curiosity.

"After the first few meetings, though, I felt a little disappointed. I'm not sure what I had expected, but there just didn't seem to be much going on. All it looked like was a group of children playing in the middle of a circle of people in wheelchairs, with one child or another occasionally wandering over to an older person to share a toy or a moment of conversation. Then I started talking with some of the staff members, and I found out that in fact there was a lot happening. I had never seen the patients when the children weren't around, so I had no base from which to make a judgment. But the staff members told me there were people in the group who never participated in any other activity—the play group period was the only time they interacted with anyone. Several of the women who watched intently, without ever saying a word, never focused on anything for more than a minute or two at any other time. When the play group was there, however, they were rapt for a solid hour. Some patients who were considered rather cranky most of the time were delighted with us. And some who were quite senile seemed to find an anchor for their mental wanderings and became quite lucid when surrounded by the children.

"For example, Molly was described to me as 'living on Mars most of the time.' She frequently must be removed from other activities because she is so disruptive and disoriented. In our play group she keeps up a running commentary, but she makes sense for the entire time we're there. If I speak to her, I might as well be a piece of furniture for all the response I get, but let a child so much as whisper in her direction and she's sharp as the proverbial tack. The children love her and she always has a lapful of toys they've taken to her to share.

"The play group has grown since we first began with three children. The group now has as many as ten or twelve, ranging in age from infancy to three. The children enjoy the play group and look forward to it. They ask about 'going to Keswick' and frequently talk about their friends there. And they see nothing peculiar or 'funny' about people in wheelchairs or old people or people with handicaps. Alan saw a woman with cerebral palsy in a shopping mall recently, announced that 'she's like Sally,' and went over to say hello. The woman was very moved; usually people try to pretend she's not there. I hope that this acceptance will always be with him.

"I know that I, too, as a result of this experience, have grown and changed in my attitudes about aging and disabilities. I think the other mothers have as well. My friend Lissa calls the play group a 'free lunch'—everybody gains and nobody pays. How many things can you say that about?"

11

How to Get Started

MY FRIEND Meg read this book and moved, she said, directly to her guilty zone because she had no wonderful new family traditions. Most people I interviewed did not have new traditions. Plenty of families on every block are warm and loving and care about each other's past, present, and future, without having inventive ways to celebrate. If we were all bursting with wonderful, satisfying new traditions, there would be no need for this book.

Traditions, old or new, are only one vehicle for giving a family definition and togetherness. If repetition doesn't work for you, don't feel guilty. If, however, you share my need for the structure and the rhythm of tradition, here is both stimulus and suggestion.

Don't procrastinate. Time has a way of surprising us with its cumulative speed. For years, it seemed we would never move beyond diapers and Dr. Seuss. Now I want to catch hold of time. "Jonathan is eleven; Seth, nine. Within the decade," I wrote in 1983, "both boys will be off to college or work and Mike and I will be shaping second-stage traditions. This period of time when the children are old enough to be a real part of our family activities, to contribute to them and enjoy them, and yet still be

· 187 ·

young enough to like cuddling and giggling with their parents, suddenly seems so short. It also seems so busy. If we don't pay attention, it slips away from us before we have established the kinds of ties that will bond us together as distance and time pull us apart."

I feel I wrote those words yesterday, yet as I sit here reviewing them, that erstwhile eleven-year-old has just received college-acceptance and draft-registration notices. The nine-year-old is now a sixteen-year-old with a brand-new driver's license who has left me holding my heart instead of my car keys. In a decade, this century will turn on twenty-six- and twenty-eight-year-old men thinking their own family thoughts.

These years have raced by. We have had our generous share of good times, but I, greedy mother that I am, wish for more—more tradition, more family time, more photos, more laughter.

It is a challenge to close the gap between the idea of a new tradition and the rooting of it in family soil. It is easy enough to do something special once or twice. Come the third time, life is a little busier, and the initial enthusiasm a little faded. Is the idea worth the work? Will it really create the feelings one wishes? Inertia exerts a powerful pull. It is easy to drift away from what drains our energy.

But there is a cost to giving in to "I just don't have the energy." With such complacency comes a graying of the internal landscape. When the future sits firmly on a solid base of good memory and experience, it is more likely to be an expansive future with space for courage and energy and possibilities.

Combat the sense of pressure that discourages us from taking time to celebrate, the sense so many of us have that we cannot stretch our time or energy one more notch, by opting for simplicity. Small moments, little gestures can have a powerful impact. A few simple but carefully chosen words like the Toums' family prayer, repeated each Thanksgiving, may be remembered far longer than the elegant menu that took hours to prepare. One of our children's most cherished traditions is waking to find "Happy Birthday" written on the bathroom mirror in toothpaste, a one-minute tradition born years ago when I couldn't find the silver birthday banner and was too tired to make a sign.

For some of us, new tradition simply means small changes in what we already do, alterations to make good traditions fit our families just a little better. For others, like a young mother I met in San Antonio, it is facing a clean slate that threatens to overwhelm us. Newly transplanted thousands of miles from family, with three small children, this woman was filled with needs and desires for her young family, but had little support. "Just how do you begin?" she asked. I don't remember what I said, but the seriousness and intensity of her question stuck with me.

Were she asking the question today, I would tell her to think of her choices as a Chinese menu. Choose one item, I would tell her, from the serious column, and one from the silly column. Begin with something that makes your family laugh: chocolate ice cream for breakfast on the first day of spring; a neighborhood midnight ramble on the longest day of summer; a back-to-school family pencil-sharpening—ten dozen at least, on Labor Day weekend, to satisfy the Abominable Pencil Eater's gluttony. Or, thrift torpedoed, buy ten dozen eggs and let the kids dye them all for Easter; declare the first week of summer vacation pizza week and let your teenagers have pizza every single night; put on a family show and spoof yourselves.

Then choose a serious tradition—something that calls on your caring or giving or reflecting selves. Volunteer for a day; write a family prayer or reach out and give to someone else, as people in this book have done; or use the ideas here as stimulus for something all your own.

Do not worry about making national holidays and major religious occasions elaborate. But define them; separate them out from other days by altering their shape and pace. Script the day so it feels special. Take a long walk, show home movies, play all your favorite tapes, watch a holiday VCR film together, play board games, read aloud, dance, go to worship, or worship at home. Fill the table with flowers or friends or favorite foods or religious symbols. Call all your relatives to wish them well; think of the ten most important events of the year for the world, the nation, the family, and write them in a family chronicle. Take pictures; tell ancestor stories. Don't try to do all these. Start with what feels most natural.

And then add one new tradition that connects you to others. Decide that every Fourth of July you and your siblings will meet, or every Thanksgiving you will fly the folks out. Start a tradition with another family—throw the I Ching every New Year's, have a Hanukkah candle-lighting and dreidel-spinning party together or share gifts and baklava to mark the end of Ramadan. There seems to be equal pleasure in sharing with those of the same culture and in being invited to share in something outside our own experience.

Try to designate one day as your time to reach out and have others in. Organize an event that is comfortable for you. If you love to cook, consider fabulous desserts on Valentine's Day. If you don't, think football and deli trays. My own entertaining strategy is to go public quickly with my plans and invite the guests. Then momentum and necessity carry me forward. If I wait until I have settled all the details, I wait right past the supposed party date.

With a silly and a serious and a social tradition taking root, a family can gradually add embellishments. They needn't come all of a piece. Once tuned to tradition, families find themselves on the lookout for particular pleasures they can institutionalize. Every time my family experiences something especially satisfying, my kids start teasing: "Well, Mom, what do you think, is this a new tradition?" The other day I yelled at them to stop horsing around and finish their homework, and back came the retort

"But, Mom, we're male-bonding." They can tease me all they want; I like having them think about tradition and bonding.

In earlier chapters, I talked about tradition having the force of habit, of coming easily because we know what to do. New traditions, of course, are not initially powered by this urge for repetition. They require energy and effort. Give them time to root.

Make a firm commitment to your new tradition and repeat it even if it feels a little forced. Comfort is seldom immediate. I remember how awkward our own Friday-night dinners felt at first. The prayers we chose were empty words. We felt self-conscious, formalizing best-thing-in-the-week thoughts. The desire to make it work kept us trying, and awkwardness left as the words became ours and the emotions took on personal significance.

Nina Holland understood when, in discussing her family's collective New Year's resolution, she said the trick was to resolve to do the possible, to set family goals the family knew it could achieve. Look for traditions that can come easily. You might begin by working to strengthen already established patterns or to resurrect, in adapted form, a bit of family past. We got to our Friday Sabbaths that way. When I first started thinking about tradition, I had the idea for an International Night on Friday. We would invite foreign students from the university and cook foreign food. I realized that required too much planning. It was easier to give our family definition by borrowing from our own cultural upbringing. Since it was a new tradition, we felt no need to apologize for shaping the past to suit our present needs.

Family brainstorming can produce some wonderful ideas, but be careful. Collective creativity may result in a tradition so elaborate that it is a production to stage. If you start off with an extravaganza and find it requires more work than anyone is willing to do again and again, just retrench down to the essentials.

Quite likely, the nub of the idea will take, even if the embellishments get a little ragtag. Again, that Friday Sabbath is an example. We started fancy. The boys put on dress shirts, Michael left on his coat and tie, and I got out good china and fancy place mats. Somewhere along the way, we lost the energy for these graces, but the candle lighting and event sharing are firmly rooted, no longer new traditions, but easy old ones.

Sometimes the opposite happens. A small beginning grows. Flourishes and expansions are added from time to time, and some stick. Find a pattern that pleases you, a rhythm that gives the day its own momentum over the years, and let it take its course.

In making a case for new tradition, I emphasized the value of continuity and the comfort of repetition. Just as newness and tradition are a contradiction, I want to introduce another contradiction: repetition and flexibility. Some new traditions will only work for a period of time. We pass through different stages in the family cycle, and each cycle makes different demands and offers different opportunities. I think of Maria's Good-Morning Stories tradition, "not a tradition likely to continue through the years just as it is." But for the thousand mornings in which it fits, it established important feelings of closeness and order that may spawn other new traditions.

Some new traditions become part of a family's heritage. The children will introduce them to their spouses and their children. But not every new tradition is forever. Something wonderful that happens just a few times can imprint powerful memories that satisfy our need to recollect long after a particular celebration ceases. In the search for traditions, in simply questioning what values we hold dear and how we might give tangible meaning to those values, there is great good. Ideas that don't take hold are not failures but simply singular events, good enough for the moment. Give yourself points just for trying.

Some years, circumstances disrupt our patterns. We all have these difficult years. Don't berate yourself for imagined failures in hard times. And don't think of the tradition as "broken," but rather as interrupted. After the pause, pick the tradition up, to continue or adapt if it still pleases you.

Building family tradition, at its best, involves the whole family. If warmth, togetherness, and family definition are a goal, simply sitting down to talk about traditions moves you toward that goal. No idea, seriously offered, is bad, but all ideas aren't equally feasible. The trick is not to put down ideas that feel improbable but to focus on the ones all members of the family are attracted to. Sometimes you don't have to choose one idea over another. Remember the Christmas story about the brothers who loved the traditional red-ribboned tree and their sisters who wanted a new-style, handcrafted tree? They had two trees. That is creative compromise.

It also worked because the people who felt the need for change accepted the responsibility of implementing the change. Those who feel strongly about how things should be can expect to do most of the work. On the other hand, those who love us should indulge and support us.

Don't be too disappointed if others do not share your enthusiasms right off. Have you ever noticed how uncooperative people can be when someone is trying to organize a family photo—and then everyone wants a copy?

Families in this book are shown in a good light. Generally, they are healthy families, but I am sure that they, too, argue, yell at their kids, and have awful moments from time to time. For some families, things like that come more frequently. My friend Ariana is married to a not very nice man who has a special talent for spoiling family events. Either he is too busy to participate, dampening the mood, or he comes and is a curmudgeon. Chip has a different sort of problem. He is a nurturer who fusses and frets over family things. His wife, whom he adores, has no need for ceremony. Already pulled in multiple directions, she is almost hostile to any new activity.

Ariana deals mostly internally with her problem. "I decided to stop letting my husband's absences spoil my mood . . . I wish it could be otherwise, but I have got to make the best of what we have. If I am at peace inside myself, if I can have fun and not just pretend, the children pick up on it. I let them know I am sorry Daddy cannot share the same kinds of pleasures, but I tell them the pleasures are still there to enjoy."

Chip's solution is external. He has built a network of celebration-loving friends who include him and his family. He rewards and encourages this with flowers, champagne, clever gifts, and other small gestures of thoughtfulness that endear him to his friends.

It is easier, gentler on our minds, if a whole family tackles traditions, but it is possible to go it alone. Especially, then, choose traditions that satisfy you, not traditions you feel obligated to carry out.

If something here fits, take it; it's yours. If it needs tailoring to fit you, nip and tuck away. And if you have been stimulated to develop your own new traditions, it would give me great pleasure to hear about them. Light the candles, lift your voice in song or shout or prayer, kiss the kids, and celebrate!

Sharing: A Space for Your Best Ideas

Dear Reader:

You have discovered that this is a recipe book of family traditions. Chefs collect recipes wherever they find something delicious, special, or inventive. They swap with friends, clip from magazines, collect cookbooks, taste, and experience.

The way to collect new traditions is to talk with people everywhere, to pry behind condominium doors and Tudor façades and suburban shrubs and farm fences. It is to ask: What do you do in your family that makes you especially you, specially Smiths or Joneses or Poldowskis, O'Connors, Chans, Epsteins, or Bommaritos or . . . ?

I cannot come to all of you, but I know there are many more special new traditions out there. I hope that you will come to me and write me about your favorite family tradition. Send one or three or however many you want. Tell me what you do and how it feels and why you do it. Tell me a little about your family if you like. If you don't like to write, tell me on a tape.

If you feel comfortable including a name, address, and phone number, I would like that. My mailing address is:

Susan Abel Lieberman
Author of *New Traditions*
c/o Farrar, Straus and Giroux
19 Union Square West, New York, NY 10003

Collecting new traditions has enriched our own family life, and I am eager to hear from people throughout the United States and from other countries as well.

Warmly,
Susan Abel Lieberman

Share *NEW TRADITIONS* with Friends and Family

Yes, I want to share *New Traditions*.
Please send *New Traditions* to the people indicated below.

QUANTITY	ISBN	TITLE	UNIT COST	TOTAL
	374522626	NEW TRADITIONS	$7.95	
Shipping & Handling (Add $3.50 for first book, 50¢ for each additional book sent to the same address.)				
			TOTAL	

SHIP TO (Add additional names on separate sheet.)

Name

Address

City, State, & Zip

CHARGE TO

Name

Address

City, State & Zip

☐ Check enclosed for _____ , payable to FSG

☐ Charge to my credit card

☐ Phone orders, call 1-800-631-8571; use code NEW

ACCT #

☐ Mastercard ☐ Visa ☐ American Express   Exp. date _____

Signature _____

Mail to: Farrar, Straus & Giroux
Sales Dept.
19 Union Square West
New York, NY 10003

Code NEW